A Wedding Ceremony to Remember

PERFECT WORDS FOR THE PERFECT WEDDING

As I have given you
my hand to hold,
so I give you
my life to keep . . .

A WORD PLANNER FOR CREATING AN
ELOQUENT, UNIQUE, AND COMPLETE WEDDING CEREMONY

Marty Younkin

BROWN BOOKS PUBLISHING GROUP
DALLAS, TEXAS

A Wedding Ceremony to Remember

PERFECT WORDS FOR THE PERFECT WEDDING

Marty Younkin

Fourth Edition
©2008 by Love Notes

BROWN BOOKS
PUBLISHING GROUP
DALLAS, TEXAS

Edited by Carol Sage
Cover design and interior layout by Beth Schmidt, BN design

First Edition Copyright 2000. Second Edition Copyright 2003. Third Edition Copyright 2005.
Fourth Edition Copyright 2008

ISBN 1482553872
ISBN 9781482553871

Love Notes
www.lovenotesweddings.com

DEDICATION

This book is lovingly dedicated to our parents, Delano and Mildred Younkin and Bud and Arline Moser. These two couples exemplified the true meaning and beauty of marriage through their commitment to love "till death do us part." It was their love and dedication to each other that helped us find the perfect words for the perfect wedding. If you could know them as we do, you would discover their recipe for a lasting marriage is found in the following acrostic:

Inspire warmth

Listen to each other
Open your heart
Value your union
Express your trust

Yield to good sense
Overlook mistakes
Understand differences

$\mathscr{P}$REFACE

Over the years, it has been my great privilege and joy to meet with hundreds of couples to discuss one of the most important events of their lives—their wedding. For each Bride and Groom, this day should always be a day to remember, a day to cherish forever, a day that will reflect the journey of love that has brought them to this moment of commitment. The wedding ceremony is, therefore, a special time of joyous celebration for the union being created between this man and this woman.

The one who presides over this occasion should acknowledge his assignment as a sacred trust. The Officiant should do his utmost to make the ceremony reflect the individuality and uniqueness of each couple who stands before him. All too often, the words shared fall into the category of "one size fits all," words that simply lose the sentiment of being "uniquely you."

A Wedding Ceremony to Remember is not just another wedding planner, but rather, a word planner. The purpose of this book is to help you select the words you want spoken on this special day. Having officiated weddings for many years, I am aware there are literally hundreds of vows, readings, blessings, and traditions from which to choose. Also, I recognize your time is valuable, and planning a wedding can be very stressful and time-consuming. Therefore, I have put together the distilled essence of what I consider to be the "best of the best."

As you spend time, energy, and money in preparing for your wedding, keep in mind the words spoken at your ceremony are, indeed, the "main event," and should be an expression of your unique relationship. Choose these words carefully, so your wedding truly will be...

A Wedding Ceremony to Remember

INTRODUCTION

Dear Bride and Groom,

Your wedding is one of the most important moments in your life. You will devote a lot of time and energy to make this a day to cherish. Your wedding also is an expensive event considering all the costs of the wedding gown, formal wear, bridal portraits and pictures, not to mention flowers, catering, cakes, reception, music, invitations, and chapel rental.

Because all these things require so much time, it is possible to overlook what I call the main event—the wedding ceremony itself, the part you and your guests will remember. A wedding is much like a Broadway production. You may have the best actors, best costumes, best sets, and best music, but if the script is mediocre, the play will be a flop. While all these other elements are important, the "script" must be the most important element for your wedding ceremony to be a success. Most couples rely on the justice of the peace, minister, priest, or rabbi to select the words for their special moment. But do you let the sales consultant select your gown, the baker select your cake, or the musicians select your music? Of course not! Then why not choose the words you want spoken at your wedding! Each ceremony contains the following elements, which are interchangeable:

Welcome	*Explanation of the Rings*
Consent	*Ring Exchange Vows*
Address	*Unity Candle (or other tradition)*
Readings	*Wedding Prayer / Blessing*
Wedding Vows	*Pronouncement*

From my years of experience as a wedding officiant, I compiled what I consider the very best of a variety of ceremonies or "scripts" for your consideration. In this book, you will find the following:

9 Wedding Ceremonies	*12 Wedding Traditions and Special Touches*
12 Readings	*12 Wedding Ceremony Formations*
12 Wedding Vows	*Ceremony Order of Service/Program Samples*
12 Ring Exchange Vows	*Wedding Rehearsal Worksheets*
12 Prayers and Blessings	*Personalized Wedding Ceremony Worksheets*

Go ahead! Make your wedding ceremony unique to you. Choose the words that fit you best, or "mix and match" to suit your needs. My desire is that this book will help you create…

A Wedding Ceremony to Remember

Marty Younkin

TABLE OF CONTENTS

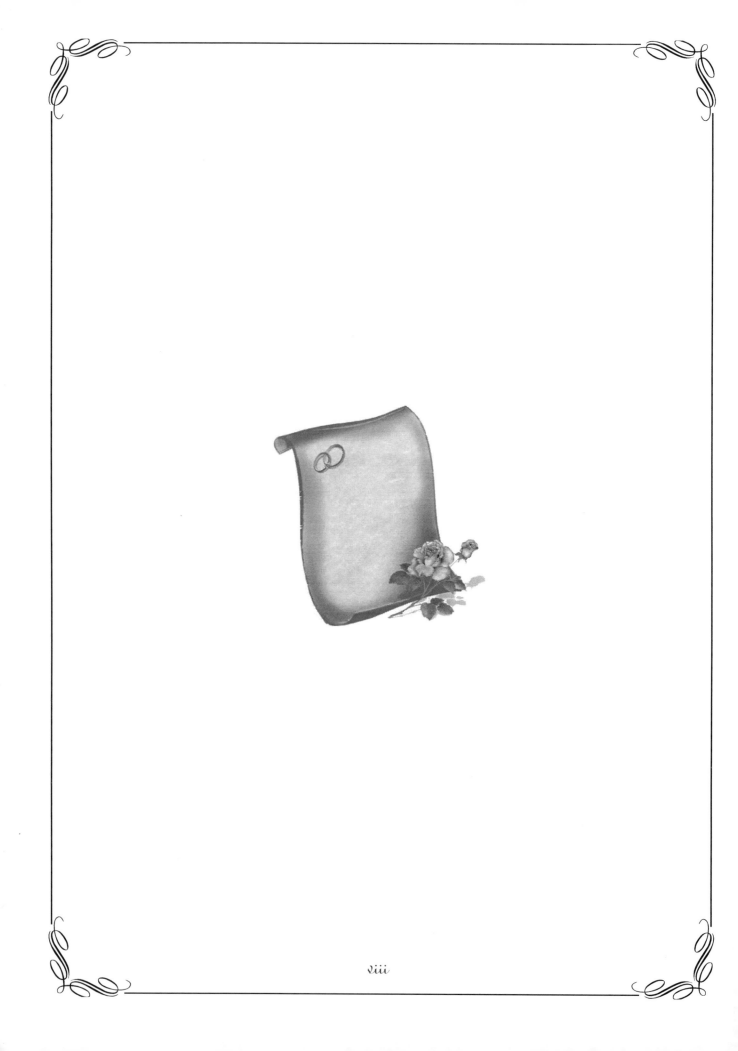

Wedding Ceremonies

*Dearly beloved, we have gathered
together in the presence of God...*

Traditional Ceremony

(Religious)

Approximate Time: 16-19 minutes
With music, entrance, and exit: 26-34 minutes

TRADITIONAL CEREMONY

WELCOME

We welcome all of you here today as we have gathered together in the presence of God and these witnesses to join (Groom's full name) _____ and (Bride's full name) _____ in holy matrimony. Marriage is a gift, a gift from God, given to us so that we might experience the joys of unconditional love with a lifelong partner. God designed marriage to be an intimate relationship between a man and a woman—mentally, emotionally, physically, and spiritually. Just as the two of you make vows to one another today, God also made vows to you and me that show how much He loves and cares for each one of us. Listen to these vows God made that are recorded for us in His Word: *"I will betroth you to myself forever in lawful wedlock with unfailing devotion and love; I will commit myself to you, to have and to hold, and you shall know the Lord."* (Groom) _____ and (Bride) _____, because your deep love for each other comes from God above, this is a sacred moment, and it is with great reverence that I now ask you to declare your intent.

CONSENT

(Groom) _____, do you take (Bride) _____ to be your wedded wife, to live together after God's ordinance in the holy estate of matrimony? Do you promise to love her, comfort her, honor and keep her, in sickness and in health, and forsaking all others, remain faithful to her as long as you both shall live?

(The Groom shall say): **I do.**

And (Bride) _____, do you take (Groom) _____ to be your wedded husband, to live together after God's ordinance in the holy estate of matrimony? Do you promise to love him, comfort him, honor and keep him, in sickness and in health, and forsaking all others, remain faithful to him as long as you both shall live?

(The Bride shall say): **I do.**

Who gives (Bride) _____ to be married to (Groom) _____?

(The Escort shall say): **Her Mother and I** or **I do** or **We do** or **Her family** or other.

(Bride gives bouquet to Maid of Honor.)

ADDRESS AND READINGS

Today is the beginning of a new life together for you. It marks the commencement of new relationships to your families, your friends, and certainly to each other. You have invited these special guests to share in one of life's greatest moments as they give recognition to the worth and beauty of your love and add their best wishes to the words that shall unite you today as husband and wife. God knew your needs when He brought you together. He knew exactly what you needed to make you complete. And now, He wants you to commit yourselves to each other as the one He has chosen to complete you.

God said, *"It is not good for man to be alone. I will make a helper suitable for him."* And so…

The Creation of Woman from the Rib of Man

The Lord God caused the man to fall into a deep sleep;
>   and while he was sleeping, He took one of the man's ribs,
>   and then closed up the place with flesh.
Then the Lord God formed a woman
>   from the rib He had taken out of the man,
>   and brought her to him.
The man said, "This is now bone of my bones
>   and flesh of my flesh;
>   she shall be called Woman, for she was taken out of Man."

Genesis 2: 21-23

Woman was made of a rib out of the side of Man.
>   She was not created from Man's head to rule over him,
>   nor from his feet to be trampled upon by him.
Instead, Woman was taken from his side, to be equal with him;
>   under his arm, to be protected;
>   and near his heart, to be loved. *(Reading #3)*

(Groom) _____, God's Word tells us what kind of husband a man should be for his wife.

"And you husbands, show the same kind of love to your wives as Christ showed to the church when He died for her. That is how husbands should be toward their wives, loving them in the same kind of way. For since a man and his wife are now one, a man is really doing himself a favor and loving himself when he loves his wife! No one hates his own body but lovingly cares for it just as Christ cares for His body, the church, of which we are all parts. Husbands, live with your wives in an understanding way, giving them respect, and treating them with honor since they are heirs together with you in the grace of life."

(Reading #11a)

(Bride) _____, the qualities that make a woman truly beautiful have been written in the book of Proverbs.

"If you can find a truly good wife, she is worth more than precious gems! Her husband can trust her, and she will richly satisfy his needs. She will not hinder him, but help him all her life. She is a woman of strength and dignity, and has no fear of old age. When she speaks, her words are wise, and kindness is the rule of everything she says. She watches carefully all that goes on throughout her household, and is never lazy. Her children stand and bless her; so does her husband. He praises her with these words: 'There are many fine women in the world, but you are the best of them all!' Charm can be deceptive and beauty doesn't last, but a woman who fears and reverences God shall be greatly praised."

(Reading #11b)

Through the ages, man has tried to define "love." Poems, songs, and books all have been written trying to describe this little four letter word. But the best description I have found comes from God Himself, since He is the Author of love. In His Word, there is a chapter commonly known as the "Love Chapter"—1 Corinthians 13. It describes the kind of love that must characterize your lives if you are to live in joy and harmony and honor with each other, and also before God and your fellow man. Listen to what it says:

> *"Love is patient and kind; love is not jealous or boastful; it is not arrogant or rude. Love does not insist on its own way; it is not irritable or resentful; it does not rejoice at wrong, but rejoices in the right. Love bears all things, believes all things, hopes all things, endures all things. Love never fails. So faith, hope, and love abide, these three; but the greatest of these is love."*
>
> *(Reading #12, Version 1–Traditional)*

(Groom) _____, I believe you are saying to all of us today that you are committing yourself to this woman only, moving toward her in a more open and intimate way, giving yourself to care for her, and promising to love her as she needs to be loved. And (Bride) _____, I believe you are saying to us that you are committing yourself to this man only, moving toward him with increasing openness, tenderness, and respect, giving yourself to him, and trusting him as the head of your home, and, through him, listening to God's plan for your life together.

And so, (Groom) _____, if you will love (Bride) _____ as Christ loves the church, and (Bride) _____, if you will respond to (Groom) _____ as unto the Lord, your companionship as husband and wife will blossom into a physical, emotional, and spiritual closeness beyond which nothing can compare.

WEDDING VOWS

(The Officiant shall say): (Groom) _____, please repeat after me.

I, (Groom) _____, take thee, (Bride) _____, / to be my wedded wife, / to have and to hold / from this day forward, / for better, for worse, / for richer, for poorer, / in sickness and in health, / to love and to cherish, / till death do us part. / This is my solemn vow. *(Wedding Vow #12)*

(The Officiant shall say): (Bride) _____, please repeat after me.

I, (Bride) _____, take thee, (Groom) _____, / to be my wedded husband, / to have and to hold / from this day forward, / for better, for worse, / for richer, for poorer, / in sickness and in health, / to love and to cherish, / till death do us part. / This is my solemn vow. *(Wedding Vow #12)*

EXPLANATION OF THE RINGS

The wedding ring serves as a symbol of the promise you have just spoken. It is the outward and visible sign of an inward and invisible love that binds your two hearts together. The wedding ring also is a symbol of what God is. He is without beginning and without end—He is eternal. As you can see, the ring is without beginning and without end. So I believe this exchange of rings not only reminds us of the unending love you have for each other, but also reflects the eternal love God has for each of you.

RING EXCHANGE VOWS

(The Officiant shall say): May I have the token of (Groom's) _____ love for (Bride) _____?
(Officiant receives ring from Best Man. Groom places ring on Bride's finger.)

(The Officiant shall then say): (Groom) _____, please repeat after me.

This ring I give in token and pledge / as a sign of my love and devotion. / With this ring, I thee wed.
(Ring Vow #10)

(The Officiant shall say): May I have the token of (Bride's) _____ love for (Groom) _____?
(Officiant receives ring from Maid of Honor. Bride places ring on Groom's finger.)

(The Officiant shall then say): (Bride) _____, please repeat after me.

This ring I give in token and pledge / as a sign of my love and devotion. / With this ring, I thee wed.
(Ring Vow #10)

LIGHTING OF THE UNITY CANDLE
(Or Other Optional Wedding Tradition)

The Unity Candle is a symbol of the union that exists between a man and a woman who enter the holy estate of matrimony. They are no longer two, but one. The Holy Bible says, *"For this cause shall a man leave his father and mother, and shall cleave to his wife, and the two shall become one flesh."* In a marriage relationship, a man and a woman leave one home to establish another. These two candles represent the individual homes in which (Groom) _____ and (Bride) _____ grew up. The center candle represents the new home they are establishing today with Christ as the heart of that home. As (Groom) _____ and (Bride) _____ join together in lighting this Unity Candle, may we all reflect on the union made here this day between God, this woman, and this man.

WEDDING PRAYER/BLESSING

Our Heavenly Father, we ask Your blessing upon these two lives and the home they are establishing today. May the love they have for each other grow deeper and stronger because of their love for You. Lord, You guided them to each other, now guide them in this new journey as husband and wife. As they walk down this path, light their way so they may keep their eyes focused on Your will, their hands holding fast to Your truth, their feet firmly planted in Your Word, and their hearts bound together by Your love. This we pray in Your name. Amen. *(Prayer #7)*

PRONOUNCEMENT

(Groom) _____ and (Bride) _____, since you have consented together in holy matrimony, and have pledged yourselves to each other by your solemn vows and by the giving of rings, and have declared your commitment of love before God and these witnesses, I now pronounce you husband and wife in the name of the Father and the Son and the Holy Spirit. Those whom God hath joined together, let no man separate.

KISS

(The Officiant shall say): (Groom) _____, you may kiss your Bride.

(Bride and Groom kiss.)

(Bride receives bouquet from Maid of Honor.)

PRESENTATION

(The Officiant shall say): Ladies and Gentlemen, it is my privilege to introduce to you for the very first time, (Mr. and Mrs.) _____.

Contemporary Ceremony

(Religious)

Approximate Time: 17-20 minutes
With music, entrance, and exit: 27-35 minutes

CONTEMPORARY CEREMONY

WELCOME

Friends and family of the Bride and Groom, we are here today because love has gathered us together. On this day, (Groom's full name) _____ and (Bride's full name) _____ will pledge their lives as one, and commit themselves to each other forever in marriage. (Groom) _____ and (Bride) _____, there are no obligations on earth more sweet or tender than those you are about to assume. There are no vows more solemn than those you are about to make. There is no human institution more sacred than that of the home you are about to establish. Marriage is the holiest of all earthly relationships. Yes, marriages are made in heaven, but they have to be maintained here on earth. May you see that your love is truly a gift from God. And may your marriage be such that all will know of your deep love for one another, as well as for God, the One who brought you together.

CONSENT

(Groom) _____, will you have (Bride) _____ to be your wife, to live together in the bonds of marriage? Will you commit yourself completely to her and her alone? And will you promise to love her, care for her, and stand by her through all that life may bring, as long as you both shall live?

(The Groom shall say): **I will.**

And (Bride) _____, will you have (Groom) _____ to be your husband, to live together in the bonds of marriage? Will you commit yourself completely to him and him alone? And will you promise to love him, care for him, and stand by him through all that life may bring, as long as you both shall live?

(The Bride shall say): **I will.**

Who presents (Bride) _____ to be married to (Groom) _____?

(The Escort shall say): **Her Mother and I** or **I do** or **We do** or **Her family** or other.

(Bride gives bouquet to Maid of Honor.)

ADDRESS AND READINGS

Today is the beginning of an exciting new life together for the two of you, (Groom) _____ and (Bride) _____. It marks the commencement of new relationships to your families, your friends, and certainly to each other. God knew your needs when He brought you together. He knew exactly what you needed to make you complete. Now He wants you to commit yourselves to each other as the one He has chosen to complete you. Total completeness, however, is a process that takes patience, perseverance, and particular principles that must be practiced so you can achieve the oneness God intended for your marriage. Here are five little "pearls of wisdom" I want to share with you as you begin this new partnership on your journey to total completeness.

First, **LISTEN**. Listen to each other. Try to hear what your mate is really saying. The Scripture says, *"Be quick to hear and slow to speak."* That's why God gave us two ears and only one mouth, so we would talk less and listen more. Take the words you hear from each other into your heart and let them become building blocks for a happy marriage. Communication is vitally important in marriage, so yes, take the time to talk with each other. But more importantly, take the time to listen to each other, for in listening, you communicate that you value your partner's thoughts and feelings.

Second, **LEARN**. Learn from each other. Both of you are different in many ways. You each bring certain abilities and specific gifts into this relationship. Learn what those talents are. Don't see them as competition; rather, accept each other's strengths and combine them with yours to become a better team. Every day will be an adventure as you learn and understand something new about your mate. In fact, the Bible says, *"Husbands, live with your wives in an understanding way."* So, (Groom) _____, your lifelong assignment is to try to understand this woman, and (Bride) _____, your lifelong assignment is to make sure he understands you. What an assignment! If you learn from each other, not only will you be better individuals, but also a better couple. So take time to learn all you can about each other.

Listen, Learn, and third, **LABOR**—or work. Be willing to work on your relationship. Make every effort to make this the very best marriage on God's earth. You don't find precious gems just lying around on top of the ground. You have to work hard to get to them. But once you find them, they are worth every bit of effort you made. So too, if you work on your marriage relationship, it will be like finding those precious gems, and because of all your labor, you will "strike it rich."

Listen, Learn, Labor, and fourth, **LAUGH**. Learn to laugh. Laugh at yourself and laugh at each other. Getting married is a serious step, and it should be taken seriously. But I am also serious when I say that having fun and being able to laugh at our mistakes and shortcomings goes a long way in solidifying the mortar of this institution we call marriage. The Bible says that *"laughter is good medicine."* Studies show that laughter has a profound and positive effect on the body. Laughter is the best medicine for a long and happy life. I guess it can be said that he who laughs . . . is the one who lasts.

Listen, Learn, Labor, Laugh, and finally, **LOVE**. What is love? Countless songs have been sung about it. Poems too many to number have been penned describing it. Books as numerous as the stars in the sky have been authored by both men and women trying to help us understand this little four letter word. But the one Book that rises above them all, the Bible, simply defines love this way:

> *"Love is very patient and kind, never jealous or envious, never boastful or proud, never haughty or selfish or rude. Love does not demand its own way nor is it irritable or touchy. It does not hold grudges and will hardly ever notice when others do it wrong. It is never glad about injustice, but rejoices whenever truth wins out. This kind of love knows no boundaries to its tolerance, no end to its trust, no fading of its hope, no limit to its endurance. It can outlast anything. Love is, in fact, the one thing that still stands when all else has failed."*
>
> *(Reading #12, Version 2–Contemporary)*

So you can see, love is not just something you feel, it is something you do. (Groom) _____, it has been said, "If you treat your wife like a queen, she will treat you like a king." Or to put it another way, "If you treat her like a thoroughbred, she'll never turn into an old nag." ☺

And so . . . **LISTEN, LEARN, LABOR, LAUGH,** and **LOVE**. Practice these five principles and, with God's guidance, your marriage will blossom and grow into a life-long partnership that will endure the challenges of life and withstand the tests of time.

WEDDING VOWS

(The Officiant shall say): (Groom) _____, please repeat after me.

(Bride) _____, I thank God He has given us to each other / to share one life, one love, one heart. / With God's help, / I will try to be everything / that He wants me to be for you, / so I may meet your needs / and fulfill your dreams. / I will love you with an unconditional love / just as Christ loves us. / In love I will lead you, / protect and provide for you, / nurture and care for you, / and honor and respect you. / I promise to stay by your side / no matter what circumstances life may bring, / and I vow to be faithful and true / to you alone. / May my love give you strength all the days of our lives.

(Wedding Vow #1a)

(The Officiant shall say): (Bride) _____, please repeat after me.

(Groom) _____, as we become husband and wife today, / I promise to love you with an unending love. / I give myself in all things to your care, / as unto the Lord. / As God has prepared me / to be your helpmate and companion in this life, / I commit myself to stand by you / whatever comes our way. / I will be with you in sickness and in health, / whether we are rich or poor, / and during times of happiness, / as well as times of sorrow. / I will honor and respect you, / encourage and support you, / and devote myself to you. / I promise to be faithful and true / to you alone. / May my love bring you joy all the days of our lives.

(Wedding Vow #1b)

EXPLANATION OF THE RINGS

You are about to give to each other a ring. The wedding ring is a symbol of many things. It is made of precious metals that symbolize a love that is pure and enduring. It is made of rare gems that symbolize a love that is priceless and irreplaceable. It is made in a perfect circle that symbolizes a love that is permanent and everlasting. Whenever you look at this ring, may it forever remind you of the promises you have made this day to keep your love pure, priceless, and permanent.

RING EXCHANGE VOWS

(The Officiant shall say): May I have the token of (Groom's) _____ love for (Bride) _____?
(Officiant receives ring from Best Man. Groom places ring on Bride's finger.)

(Officiant shall then say): (Groom) _____, please repeat after me.

_____, I give you this ring / as a symbol of my love and faithfulness, / and as I ⟶ / I commit my very heart and soul to you. / I ask you to wear this ring / as a ⟶ve spoken / on this, our wedding day. *(Ring Vow #2)*

⟶ken of (Bride's) _____ love for (Groom)_____?
⟶ Bride places ring on Groom's finger.)

_____, please repeat after me.

⟶ you this ring / as a sign of my commitment / and the desire of my ⟶der / that I have chosen you above all others, / and from this day ⟶s husband and wife. *(Ring Vow #3)*

LIGHTING OF THE UNITY CANDLE
(Or Other Optional Wedding Tradition)

Lighting the Unity Candle is a symbol of the union created by a man and a woman who enter into marriage. They are no longer two, but one. The Bible says, *"For this cause a man shall leave his father and mother, and shall cleave to his wife, and the two shall become one flesh."* Today, we see two people uniting themselves as one—as one in the flesh and as one in the spirit. These candles symbolize that union. The two outer candles represent the individual lives of (Groom) _____ and (Bride) _____ and the families from which they came. The lighting of this Unity Candle not only symbolizes the coming together of these two individuals, but the joining together of their families, as well. May you all recognize your continuing importance in each other's lives by sharing with each other the light of your love.

WEDDING PRAYER/BLESSING

Dear Lord, we pray that You will bless this man and this woman as they begin their new journey together. In all the experiences of life, may they always stay close to You and to each other as they share the joys and blessings, as well as the trials and heartaches. Help them to honor and keep the promises made here today. Remind them daily of Your great love for them so they, in turn, may reach out in love to others. Give them such love and devotion that each may be to the other a strength in need, a comfort in sorrow, a counselor in difficulty, and a companion in joy. Amen. *(Prayer #9)*

PRONOUNCEMENT

(Groom) _____ and (Bride) _____, today, before your family and friends, you have openly declared your love for each other. You have joined your hands, spoken your promises, and given these rings, a symbol of your lifelong commitment to each other. And so, I now bestow upon you the most honorable titles that may exist between a man and a woman; I pronounce you husband and wife.

KISS

(The Officiant shall say): (Groom) _____, you may kiss your Bride.

(Bride and Groom kiss.)

(Bride receives bouquet from Maid of Honor.)

PRESENTATION

(The Officiant shall say): Ladies and Gentlemen, it is my privilege to introduce to you for the very first time, (Mr. and Mrs.) _____.

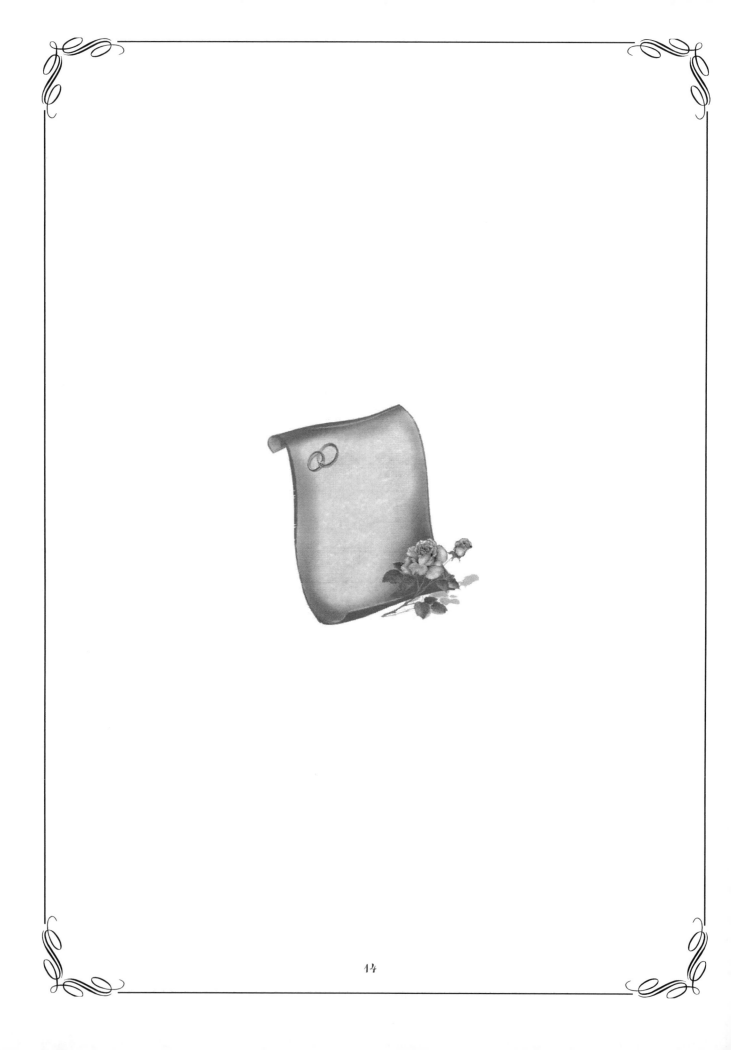

Civil Ceremony

(Non-Religious)

Approximate Time: 12-15 minutes
With music, entrance, and exit: 20-25 minutes

Civil Ceremony

WELCOME

Love is a miraculous gift, and a wedding is a celebration of that gift. We have come here today to celebrate this gift of love, and to add our best wishes and blessings to the words that shall unite (Groom's full name) _____ and (Bride's full name) _____ in the bonds of marriage. What you promise to each other today must be renewed again tomorrow and every day that follows. At the end of this ceremony, legally you will be husband and wife. Still, you must decide each and every day to commit yourselves to one another. Make such a decision, and keep on making it, for the most important thing in life is to love and to be loved.

CONSENT

(Groom) _____ and (Bride) _____, do you come here of your own free will, accompanied by your family's blessings, to be united as husband and wife forevermore?

(Both answer): **I do.**

Who presents (Bride) _____ to be married to (Groom) _____?

(The Escort shall say): **Her Mother and I** or **I do** or **We do** or **Her family** or other.

(Bride gives bouquet to Maid of Honor.)

ADDRESS AND READINGS

Today you are taking into your care and trust the happiness of the one person in this world whom you love with all your heart. And you are giving yourself, your life, and your love, into the hands of the one who loves you with all their heart. Always remember this, to the whole world, you are but one person, but to one person, you are the whole world.

However, true love goes far beyond the feelings of excitement and romance. It is caring more about the well-being and happiness of your marriage partner than your own needs and your own desires. And true love does not consist of gazing at each other, but in looking outward together in the same direction. You see, love makes burdens lighter because you divide them. Love makes joys more intense because you share them. Love makes you stronger so you can become involved with life in ways you dare not risk alone. True love says the two of you are just better together than when you are apart.

When you enter into marriage, you enter into life's most important relationship. It is a gift given to bring comfort when there is sorrow, peace when there is unrest, laughter when there is happiness, and love when it is shared. But a successful marriage is not something that just happens. It takes work, it takes understanding, and it takes time. Most importantly, it takes a commitment from both of you—a commitment to do whatever it takes to make your relationship thrive and not just simply survive. A good marriage must be nurtured. Listen to these "words of wisdom" on how to create a successful marriage from a little book entitled <u>The Art of Marriage</u>.

The Art of Marriage

The little things are the big things.

It is never being too old to hold hands.

It is remembering to say "I love you" at least once a day.

It is never going to sleep angry.

It is at no time taking the other for granted; the courtship should not end with the honeymoon, it should continue through all the years.

It is having a mutual sense of values and common objectives; it is facing the world together.

It is forming a circle of love that gathers in the whole family.

It is doing things for each other, not in the attitude of duty or sacrifice, but in the spirit of joy.

It is speaking words of appreciation and demonstrating gratitude in thoughtful ways.

It is not expecting the husband to wear a halo or the wife to have the wings of an angel.

It is not looking for perfection in each other.

It is cultivating flexibility, patience, understanding, and a sense of humor.

It is having the capacity to forgive and forget.

It is giving each other an atmosphere in which each can grow.

It is finding room for the things of the spirit.

It is the common search for the good and the beautiful.

It is the establishing of a relationship in which the independence is equal, the dependence is mutual, and the obligation is reciprocal.

And finally, it is not only marrying the right partner, it is being the right partner.

(Reading #2)

WEDDING VOWS

(The Officiant shall say): (Groom) _____, please repeat after me.

I, (Groom) _____, take you, (Bride) _____, / to be my partner in life. / I promise to walk by your side forever, / and to love, help, and encourage you / in all that you do. / I will take time to talk with you, / to listen to you, / and to care for you. / I will share your laughter and your tears / as your partner, lover, and best friend. / Everything I am and everything I have is yours / now and forevermore.

(Wedding Vow #2a)

(The Officiant shall say): (Bride) _____, please repeat after me.

I, (Bride) _____, give myself to you (Groom) _____, / on this our wedding day. / I will cherish our friendship, / and love you today, tomorrow, and forever. / I will trust you and honor you. / I will love you faithfully / through the best and the worst, / through the difficult and the easy. / Whatever comes our way, I will be there always. / As I have given you my hand to hold, / so I give you my life to keep.

(Wedding Vow #2b)

EXPLANATION OF THE RINGS

The wedding ring is a circle that has no end, and symbolizes the never-ending love that exists between you. The ring is made from precious metals purified by the heat of testing, and is a symbol of the purity of your love for one another. The ring also is made of rare gems that radiate a brilliance and a quality unlike other ordinary stones, and represents the riches that reside in each of you. May these rings always reflect the light of your love throughout your life together.

RING EXCHANGE VOWS

(The Officiant shall say): May I have the token of (Groom's) _____ love for (Bride) _____?
(Officiant receives ring from Best Man. Groom places ring on Bride's finger.)

(The Officiant shall then say): (Groom) _____, please repeat after me.

I give you this ring. / Wear it with love and joy. / As this ring has no end, / neither shall my love for you. / I choose you to be my wife / this day and forevermore. *(Ring Vow #5)*

(The Officiant shall say): May I have the token of (Bride's) _____ love for (Groom) _____?
(Officiant receives ring from Maid of Honor. Bride places ring on Groom's finger.)

(The Officiant shall then say): (Bride) _____, please repeat after me.

This ring I give you / in token of my love and devotion, / and with my heart, / I pledge to you all that I am. / With this ring, I marry you / and join my life to yours. *(Ring Vow #6)*

LIGHTING OF THE UNITY CANDLE
(Or Other Optional Wedding Tradition)

When the flames of two individual candles join together, a single brighter light is created from that union. May the brightness of this light shine throughout your lives, giving you courage and reassurance in the darkness. May its warmth give you shelter from the cold, and may its energy fill your spirits with strength and joy. Now as you light this candle, may it symbolize that today you become as one…hand in hand, heart to heart, flesh to flesh, and soul to soul.

WEDDING PRAYER/BLESSING

Now you will feel no rain, for each of you will be a shelter for the other. Now you will feel no cold, for each of you will be warmth to the other. Now there will be no loneliness, for each of you will be a companion to the other. Now you are two persons, but there is only one life before you. Go now to your dwelling place to enter the days of your togetherness. May beauty surround you both in the journey ahead and through all the years. May happiness be your companion, and may your days together be good and long upon the earth. *(Apache Blessing)*
(Blessing #2)

PRONOUNCEMENT

(Groom) _____ and (Bride) _____, because you have committed yourselves to each other in marriage, and demonstrated this by the exchanging of vows and the giving of rings, I pronounce you husband and wife.

KISS

(The Officiant shall say): (Groom) _____, you may kiss your Bride.

(Bride and Groom kiss.)

(Bride receives bouquet from Maid of Honor.)

PRESENTATION

(The Officiant shall say): Ladies and Gentlemen, it is my privilege to introduce to you for the very first time, (Mr. and Mrs.) _____.

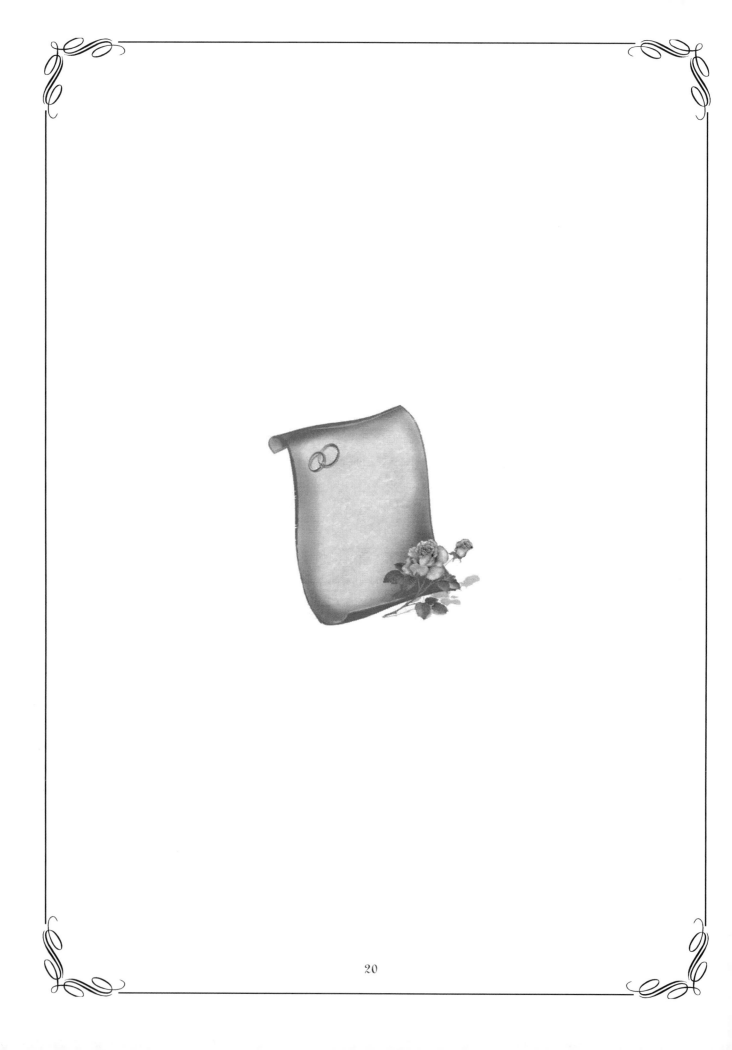

Short and Sweet Ceremony

(Non-Religious)

Approximate Time: 8-10 minutes
With music, entrance, and exit: 15-20 minutes

Short and Sweet Ceremony

WELCOME

We are here today to celebrate the miracle of love. (Groom's full name) _____ and (Bride's full name) _____ have found that miracle in each other and now desire to share their love all the days of their lives.

CONSENT

Are both of you willing to give your hand to the one whose heart you hold?

(Both answer): **Yes, we are.**

Who presents (Bride) _____ to be married to (Groom) _____?

(The Escort shall say): **Her Mother and I** or **I do** or **We do** or **Her family** or other.

(Bride gives bouquet to Maid of Honor.)

ADDRESS AND READINGS

Today you are giving yourselves to one another to love and to live. Your lives are being woven together, and in time, they will intertwine in such a way that you truly will become one in heart, mind, and soul. Listen to these words that reflect this kind of love between a man and a woman.

When a Man and a Woman Are in Love

When a man and a woman are in love,
   His life lies within hers
      and her life lies within his.
Each lives as an individual,
   yet they also live
      for one another.
Each strives for independent goals,
   but they also work together
      to achieve their dreams.
When a man and a woman are in love,
   they will give to one another
      what they need to survive
   and help fulfill each other's wants.
They will turn one another's
   disappointment into satisfaction.
They will turn one another's
   frustration into contentment.

They will work as a mirror,
   reflecting to each other
      their strengths and weaknesses.
They will work together
   to alleviate the emotional walls
      that may separate them.
They will work together to build
   a better understanding of one another.
They will learn to lean on each other,
   but not so much as to be
      a burden on the other.
They will learn to reach out to one another,
   but not so much as to suffocate the other.
They will learn when it is time to speak
   and when it is time to listen.
They will be there to comfort each other
   in times of sorrow.
They will be there to celebrate together
   in times of happiness.

They will be one another's friend,
　　guiding each other to the happiness
　　　　that life holds.
They will be one another's companion,
　　facing together the challenges
　　　　that life may present.

When a man and a woman are in love,
　　his life lies within hers
　　　　and her life lies within his.
Together they will love one another
　　for the rest of their lives
　　　　and forever.

(Reading #4)

(Groom) _____ and (Bride) _____, may this kind of love always help you keep the promises you are about to make here today.

WEDDING VOWS

(Bride/Groom) _____/_____, my promise to you is but a simple one. I will love you today and everyday that follows until the end of time. With the passing of every minute, my love grows stronger and my devotion grows deeper. I will love and cherish you until my eyes can no longer see your beauty, my ears can no longer hear your loving words, and my hands can no longer feel your tender caress. From this moment until my dying breath, you are my love—you are my life.

(Wedding Vow #6)

NOTE: These wedding vows are best if read rather than repeated.

EXPLANATION OF THE RINGS

The wedding ring is the outward and visible sign of an inward and spiritual bond that unites two loyal hearts in endless love. May these rings always remind you that it was love that brought you together, and it is love that will keep you together through all the seasons of your lives.

RING EXCHANGE VOWS

(The Officiant shall say): May I have the token of (Groom's) _____ love for (Bride)_____ ?
(Officiant receives ring from Best Man. Groom places ring on Bride's finger.)

(The Officiant shall then say): (Groom) _____, please repeat after me.

(Bride) _____, this ring is the token of my love. / I marry you with this ring, / with all that I have and all that I am. *(Ring Vow #1a)*

(The Officiant shall say): (Bride) _____, please respond by repeating after me.

(Groom) _____, I will forever wear this ring / as the sign of my commitment / and the desire of my heart. *(Ring Vow #1b)*

(The Officiant shall say): May I have the token of (Bride's) _____ love for (Groom)_____ ?
(Officiant receives ring from Maid of Honor. Bride places ring on Groom's finger.)

(The Officiant shall then say): (Bride) _____, please repeat after me.

(Groom) _____, this ring is the token of my love. / I marry you with this ring, / with all that I have and all that I am. *(Ring Vow #1a)*

(The Officiant shall say): (Groom) _____, please respond by repeating after me.

(Bride) _____, I will forever wear this ring / as the sign of my commitment / and the desire of my heart. *(Ring Vow #1b)*

LIGHTING OF THE UNITY CANDLE
(Or Other Optional Wedding Tradition)

The lighting of the Unity Candle symbolizes the joining together of your two hands, your two hearts and your two lives into one. From this moment on, the light of your love burns jointly as you walk down life's pathway together. May the path of life become brighter as the flame of your love grows stronger.

WEDDING PRAYER/BLESSING

May God bless you with Hope enough to keep sunshine in your love, and Fear enough to keep you holding hands in the dark. May God bless you with Unity enough to keep your roots entwined, and Separation enough to keep you reaching for each other. May God bless you with Harmony enough to keep romance in your song, and Discord enough to keep you tuning your love so it becomes sweet music to all who may hear it.

(Blessing #3)

PRONOUNCEMENT

(Groom) _____ and (Bride) _____, now that you have shared with each other these words of love and commitment, and we have witnessed the expression of your love as you have given each other these rings, and you have joined your hands and hearts before your family and friends, it is with great joy that I pronounce you husband and wife.

KISS

(The Officiant shall say): (Groom) _____, you may kiss your Bride.

(Bride and Groom kiss.)

(Bride receives bouquet from Maid of Honor.)

PRESENTATION

(The Officiant shall say): Ladies and Gentlemen, it is my privilege to introduce to you for the very first time, (Mr. and Mrs.) _____.

Second Time Around Ceremony

(For the previously married)

Approximate Time: 17-20 minutes
With music, entrance, and exit: 25-30 minutes

Second Time Around Ceremony

WELCOME

What a joy it is to gather here today to celebrate the rebirth of love in the hearts of two very special people, (Groom's full name) _____ and (Bride's full name) _____.
As your family and friends, we recognize that this love was sent as a precious gift through the person who is standing before you now. The love that you have found in each other has brought sunshine back into your lives once again. For you are to each other a healer of the heart, a mender of the emotions, and a source of solitude for the spirit.

CONSENT

(Groom) _____ and (Bride) _____, a new life lies before you. Are you ready to walk down this path as husband and wife, and live together in the covenant of faith, hope, and love?

(Both answer): **Yes, we are.**

Who presents (Bride) _____ to be married to (Groom) _____?

(The Escort shall say): **Her Mother and I** or **I do** or **We do** or **Her family** or other.

(Bride gives bouquet to Maid of Honor.)

ADDRESS AND READINGS

There is an old love song that captures the spirit of this wedding today. It goes like this:

The Second Time Around

Love is lovelier
  the second time around.
Just as wonderful
  with both feet on the ground.
It's that second time you hear
  your love song sung.
Makes you think, perhaps,
  that love, like youth,
    is wasted on the young.

Love's more comfortable
  the second time you fall.
Like a friendly home,
  the second time you call.
Who can say what brought us
  to this miracle we've found?
There are those who'll bet
  love comes but once, and yet,
I'm oh so glad we met
  THE SECOND TIME AROUND.

Aren't you glad God gives us a second chance? He does not want us to give up on this institution of marriage just because circumstances took love in a direction we did not anticipate. When he designed marriage, God had a special plan in mind that He wants us to embrace.

The Institution of Marriage

The institution of marriage was begun
    that a man and a woman
        might learn how to love
            and, in loving, know joy;

that a man and a woman
    might learn how to share pain and loneliness
        and, in sharing, know strength;
that a man and a woman
    might learn how to give
        and, in giving, know communion.

The institution of marriage was begun
    that a man and a woman
        might, through their joy, their strength,
            and their communion,
                become creators of life itself.

Marriage is a high and holy state,
    to be held in honor
        among all men and women.

Marriage also is a low and common state,
    to be built of the stuff
        of daily life.

Men and women are not angels, nor are they gods.
    Love can become hatred;
        joy, sorrow;
            marriage, divorce.

But human beings are not condemned to failure.
    Love can grow even in a real world.
        The wounds of sorrow can be healed,
            And new life built
                on the learnings of the old.

This is the reason for our gathering today:
    to renew our faith
        in the strength of hope
            and the power of love.

(Reading #1)

ADDRESS AND READINGS

Today, (Groom) _____ and (Bride) _____, you are beginning a new journey with the one person who means the most to you in this whole world. Remember that, to the world, you are but one person, but to one person . . . you are the world. And so, I would like to share with you three ways of looking at life as you walk through this world together.

First, I want to encourage you to look at life through the eyes of **FAITH**. It wasn't fate that brought you to this moment, it was faith—faith that you could experience life again. For when you chose to love again, you chose to live again. So today, we not only celebrate your love, but life itself. It is through faith that we are able to wipe out the old canvases of our lives and allow God, with His amazingly artistic talent, to fill them with new color, harmony, and beauty. Sometimes our lives are like a desert, seemingly void of all life; but given a little rainfall, life springs into existence. At one time, your lives may have been a desert, but through faith in God, in life, in love, and in each other, your lives have blossomed into something beautiful. So keep on looking at life through the eyes of **FAITH**.

Second, look at life through the eyes of **HOPE**. Never has hope been so alive and so strong as it is today. As you hold each other's hand right now, you are holding onto hope. And what is hope? Hope is a wish your heart makes for all your dreams to come true. This person standing before you is your "dream come true." Even when you thought love would not ever come your way again, you still dreamed of a special someone with whom to share your life. When you first met the one you are about to marry today, hope began to live again in your heart. It was this hope that enabled you to see the possibilities of a new beginning and a new life. Hope says to never give up on your dreams, for your "dream come true" may be just around the corner. So, continue to hold onto **HOPE**.

Third, look at life through the eyes of **LOVE**. You have learned a lot about love. You have even learned that sometimes love hurts. It is the painful side of love that often causes us to withdraw and retreat inside ourselves. Then we begin to build walls around our hearts. When love approaches the door to our hearts, we shut the door and keep love out. When we keep love out, we keep life out. We cease to live life the way it was meant to be lived because we haven't experienced love the way we were meant to be loved. Now, all that has changed. You both were willing to take the risk because you believed in the power of love. You chose a gift once opened and made it new again. And as a result, you rediscovered the greatest gift in life—the gift of unconditional **LOVE**. The best description of unconditional love ever written says this:

"Love is very patient and kind, never jealous or envious, never boastful or proud, never haughty or selfish or rude. Love does not demand its own way nor is it irritable or touchy. It does not hold grudges and will hardly ever notice when others do it wrong. It is never glad about injustice, but rejoices whenever truth wins out. This kind of love knows no boundaries to its tolerance, no end to its trust, no fading of its hope, no limit to its endurance. It can outlast anything. Love is, in fact, the one thing that still stands when all else has failed. These three things remain: faith, hope, and love . . . but the greatest of these is love."

1 Corinthians 13:4-7, 13 (Reading #12, Version 2—Contemporary)

WEDDING VOWS

(Bride/Groom) _____ / _____, *(Option A)* God has given us a second chance at happiness. *(Option B)* We have been given a second chance at happiness. Before I met you, I was only half a person with an emptiness in my heart. But your love has filled that void completely, and I am whole again. Today is the first day of the rest of our lives. As we begin a new life together, I promise to give my future to you in faith, my heart to you in hope, and my life to you in love. *(Wedding Vow #8)*

NOTE: These wedding vows are best if read rather than repeated.

EXPLANATION OF THE RINGS

I will now ask you to seal the vows you shared with each other by the giving and receiving of rings. The perfect circle of the ring symbolizes eternity. The precious metal is a symbol of all that is pure. It came from the ground as rough ore that had to be tried by a refiner's fire in order to melt away all the impurities. May these rings symbolize not only your eternal love for each other, but also the melting away of the past. So now, all that remains is the pure essence of your love.

RING EXCHANGE VOWS

(The Officiant shall say): May I have the token of (Groom's) _____ love for (Bride)_____ ?
(Officiant receives ring from Best Man. Groom places ring on Bride's finger.)

(The Officiant shall then say): (Groom) _____, please repeat after me.

(Bride) _____, I give you this ring / as a symbol of my love for you. / Just as this band encircles your finger, / may you always feel encircled by my love. *(Ring Vow #7)*

(The Officiant shall say): May I have the token of (Bride's) _____ love for (Groom) _____?
(Officiant receives ring from Maid of Honor. Bride places ring on Groom's finger.)

(The Officiant shall then say): (Bride) _____, please repeat after me.

(Groom) _____, I give you this ring / as a symbol of my love for you. / Just as this band encircles your finger, / may you always feel encircled by my love. *(Ring Vow #7)*

LIGHTING OF THE UNITY CANDLE
(Or Other Optional Wedding Tradition)

The lighting of the Unity Candle is a reminder that the fires of love have once again been rekindled in your hearts. Sometimes our inner light goes out, but it is blown into flame again by an encounter with another human being. Each of us owes the deepest debt of gratitude to those who have rekindled this inner light. Because the two of you are the "rekindler" of each other's flame, today you will join your inner lights into one brighter light. May the light of your lives grow and glow so others may see the flame and feel the warmth of your love.

WEDDING PRAYER/BLESSING

May your marriage be blessed with faith for the future. May your hearts be filled with the happiness of hope. May your lives be enlightened with an everlasting love. May God grant you a new beginning as He opens the door to life's deepest and richest experiences. May the life you build together be a lasting testimony that a second chance is for those who never give up believing in the power of FAITH, HOPE, and LOVE. *(Blessing #10)*

PRONOUNCEMENT

(Groom) _____ and (Bride) _____, as you exchanged vows with one another, we witnessed the miracle of faith. As you gave and received these rings, we witnessed the miracle of hope. As you seal this commitment with a kiss, we will witness the miracle of love. Sharing with you in these three miracles gives me great joy as I now pronounce you husband and wife.

KISS

(The Officiant shall say): (Groom) _____, you may kiss your Bride.

(Bride and Groom kiss.)

(Bride receives bouquet from Maid of Honor.)

PRESENTATION

(The Officiant shall say): Ladies and Gentlemen, it is my privilege to introduce to you for the very first time, (Mr. and Mrs.) _____.

All in the Family Ceremony

(For marriages with children)

Approximate Time: 18-22 minutes
With music, entrance, and exit: 27-35 minutes

All in the Family Ceremony

WELCOME

On behalf of (Groom) _____ and (Bride) _____, I would like to thank all of you for being here to share in their special day. This moment in time is truly a cause for joyous celebration, for we are here to witness not only the beginning of a new marriage, but also the beginning of a new family. Today, (Groom's full name) _____ and (Bride's full name) _____ will be united in marriage, and (Children) _____ will be entering this new family to make it complete.

CONSENT

So, (Groom) _____, (Bride) _____, and (Children) _____, are all of you ready to make a commitment to this marriage and to this new family that is beginning today?

(Groom, Bride and children answer): **Yes, we are.**

Who presents (Bride) _____ to be married to (Groom) _____?

(The Escort shall say): **Her Mother and I** or **I do** or **We do** or **Her family** or other.

(Bride gives bouquet to Maid of Honor.)

ADDRESS AND READINGS

Today, a new chapter is being written in your lives. We could call the title of this chapter, "New Beginnings." You are beginning new relationships to your family, to your friends, and to each other. You are beginning a new life together; you are beginning a new family; you are beginning a new home. As you build this new home together, remember there are three important ingredients you will need to add to the recipe we call "Marriage and Family."

The first ingredient is TIME. It is going to take time for your home to be everything you want it to be. It will take time to blend your lives together into a new family. See your new family as a beautiful rainbow with each individual person having a distinct color, each one providing a different shade to make the rainbow complete. But remember, it takes both the sun and the rain to make a rainbow, and so it will be in your relationships with one another. The rain may come and dampen things at times, but rain is necessary to make things grow. Soon, the sun will shine and bring forth the many different colored facets of your lives. In time, you will begin to see what a precious gift you have in each other—what a beautiful rainbow this family will become. So, let TIME take its time.

The second ingredient is TALK. Communication is vitally important in your relationship as a family. We live in an age of telecommunication with cell phones, fax machines, and the Internet filling our lives with "better ways" to communicate. Yet, with all this incredible technology, one of the greatest needs of a family is just simply to talk with each other. Each day, set aside some uninterrupted time with the television and the phones turned off and just sit around the table and talk. Talk about your interests, your needs, your problems, your solutions, your hopes, and your dreams. By talking and listening, you will communicate something far more important than mere words. You will communicate you care about each other. So take time to talk and take time to listen, not only to each other, but to God, as well. For it has been said, "the family that prays together, stays together."

The third ingredient is TEAMWORK. Do things together. Work together, play together, eat together, laugh together, cry together, struggle together, and pray together. You are in this together. No one person is more or less important than the other. You are a team and everyone needs to participate in the game of life. Yes, there will be some strikeouts and a few foul balls now and then. That's part of the game. But there also will be some hits, a few home runs, and maybe even a grand slam or two. These things only happen when *everyone* plays 100 percent. In a baseball game, whenever a runner gets on base, the whole purpose is to bring him around to home plate. That is what you are doing; because you are a team, you are bringing each other home.

TIME . . . TALK . . . TEAMWORK . . . If you mix these three ingredients into the daily recipe of life, then your marriage and your family will truly blend into all you want it to be. Finally, I want to share with you an old tried and true family recipe for making a happy home. It is called, "The Happy Home Recipe."

Happy Home Recipe

Start with 1 heaping house full of Humans.

Add 1 cup each: Commitment, Cooperation, Courage, Courtesy, Consideration, and Contentment.

Allow 2 cups of open and honest Communication to simmer on low heat, but never let it come to a full boil.

Pour in 1 quart Milk of Human Kindness, along with 1 can Sweetened Condensed Confidence.

Add 3 tablespoons pure extract of "I Am Sorry,"
    and mix well with a generous portion of Forgiveness, Patience, and Understanding.

Throw in a mouth full of Praise, Encouragement, and Support,
    and season with a hand full of Loyalty and Friendship.

Stir in 1 big barrel of Laughter with just a pinch of Teasing,
    and sprinkle with a pocket full of Hopes and Dreams.

Mix 1 gallon of Faith in God and Faith in each other with one heart full of Gratitude for countless blessings.

Continue to fill kettle until overflowing with Joy and Peace.

Carefully blend all the ingredients together into this big Pot of People and cook very slowly.

Remove any specks of Temper, Jealousy, or Criticism, and never serve with a Hot Tongue or a Cold Shoulder.

Sweeten well with a heapin' helpin' of Love and Tenderness,
    and always keep warm with a steady flame of Devotion.

Remember to savor the flavor of every moment,
    and if preserved with Care, this Happy Home will last a lifetime.

(Reading #10)

WEDDING VOWS

(The Officiant shall say): (Groom) _____ would like to share his vows with (Bride) _____.

I love you (Bride) _____, and I love (Children) _____ [as my very own]. Today, as we become husband and wife, we also will become a family and begin a new life together. I promise to be a faithful husband and loving father, and I will be there for you and for the children always. No matter what circumstances life may bring, with God's help, we will face them together as a family. I commit myself to each of you from this day forward and forevermore. *(Wedding Vow #9)*

(The Officiant shall say): (Bride) _____ would like to share her vows with (Groom) _____.

I love you (Groom) _____, and I love (Children) _____ [as my very own]. Today, as we become husband and wife, we also will become a family and begin a new life together. I promise to be a faithful wife and loving mother, and I will be there for you and for the children always. No matter what circumstances life may bring, with God's help, we will face them together as a family. I commit myself to each of you from this day forward and forevermore. *(Wedding Vow #9)*

NOTE: These wedding vows are best if read rather than repeated.

EXPLANATION OF THE RINGS

You are about to present a ring to each other. The wedding ring, a complete circle, is a symbol of the completeness a husband and wife find in a marriage relationship. The ring has no beginning and no end, just as true love is never-ending. The ring also is made of precious metals and precious gems, just as true love is a precious treasure. As you place the wedding ring on each other's hand, may it not only remind you of the endless love you possess for one another, but may it also be a reminder of the precious gift God has given you to make you complete.

RING EXCHANGE VOWS

(The Officiant shall say): May I have the token of (Groom's) _____ love for (Bride) _____?
(Officiant receives ring from Best Man. Groom places ring on Bride's finger.)

(The Officiant shall then say): (Groom) _____, please repeat after me.

(Bride) _____, as I place this ring on your finger, / may it always remind you / of my never-ending love, / and may it always remind me / of the precious treasure I have in you. / Wear this ring with joy, / for your love has made me complete. *(Ring Vow #4)*

(The Officiant shall say): May I have the token of (Bride's) _____ love for (Groom) _____?
(Officiant receives ring from Maid of Honor. Bride places ring on Groom's finger.)

(The Officiant shall then say): (Bride) _____, please repeat after me.

(Groom) _____, as I place this ring on your finger, / may it always remind you / of my never-ending love, / and may it always remind me / of the precious treasure I have in you. / Wear this ring with joy, / for your love has made me complete. *(Ring Vow #4)*

CELEBRATION OF THE NEW FAMILY

When a couple marries, it is not just the joining of two lives together, it is the coming together of families, as well. This is especially true today. For as (Groom) _____ and (Bride) _____ become husband and wife, they also are joined now by (Children) _____ to become a family. At this time, we recognize these children [this child] and acknowledge their [his/her] significance on this wedding day.

COMMITMENT TO THE CHILDREN

(The children shall come forward and form a circle with the Bride and Groom. They may all join hands as the Bride and Groom read the following vows to the children):

Today, as we become husband and wife, we welcome you, (Children) _____ into our new family. We recognize you are a precious gift from God. We promise to be there for you always, to comfort you and care for you, to protect you and provide for you, to guide you and listen to you, and most of all, to love you with all of our hearts all the days of our lives.

PRESENTATION OF GIFTS

Just as (Groom) _____ and (Bride) _____ gave each other rings as symbols of their love and commitment to one another, they also would like to present [each of] you with a gift as a symbol of their love and commitment to you. *(At this time, the Bride and Groom present their gifts, such as pins or rings, medals or medallions, and give each child a hug and a kiss.)*

If the gift is the Family Medallion®, the Officiant will explain the significance of its three conjoined circles by saying): The Family Medallion® is made up of three intertwining circles, two of which symbolize the union of this man and woman in marriage. The third circle represents the joining of children to this union, making it complete as we celebrate the new family created here today. (To order the Family Medallion®, go to www.lovenotesweddings.com.)

LIGHTING OF THE FAMILY UNITY CANDLE
(Optional)

OPTION A

The Groom's children jointly light the Groom's candle and the Bride's children jointly light the Bride's candle. Then the Bride and Groom take their respective candles and jointly light the Unity Candle.

OPTION B

The Bride and Groom light the Unity Candle first with their individual candles, then take the Unity Candle and together light each child's candle from that flame.

OPTION C

The Bride and Groom light each child's candle with their individual candles, and together they all light the Unity Candle as a family.

You will need candles for the Bride, Groom, and each child represented, in addition to the Unity Candle.

The lighting of the Family Unity Candle symbolizes the blending together of two homes into one home, two families into one family, (number of family members) _____ hearts into one heart, and many colors into one rainbow. Just as you light your candles together, so may your love for each other light up your lives, both individually and together as a family.

WEDDING PRAYER/BLESSING

May God bless your [this] marriage and family as you [they] create a new home together. A family is a circle of strength and love. With every birth and every union, the circle grows. May every joy shared also add love to the circle, and may every crisis faced together make the circle even stronger. May your [this] family become like a beautiful rainbow as each color of your [their] lives is carefully blended together with both the showers and the sunshine of God's love. Amen. *(Blessing #11)*

PRONOUNCEMENT

(Groom) _____ and (Bride) _____, because you have committed yourselves to each other and to these children, and because you have proclaimed your love for each other and for these children by the giving and receiving of rings and these gifts, I now pronounce you husband and wife and family.

KISS

(The Officiant shall say): (Groom) _____, you may kiss your Bride.

(Bride and Groom kiss.)

(Bride receives bouquet from Maid of Honor.)

PRESENTATION

(The Officiant shall say): Ladies and Gentlemen, it is my privilege to introduce to you for the very first time, (Mr. and Mrs.) _____ and family.

– OR –

It is my pleasure to present to you (Groom) _____ and (Bride) _____ in their new relationship as husband and wife, and their son / daughter / children _____.

– OR –

May I present to you the _____ family.

Interfaith Ceremony

(Jewish - Christian)

Approximate Time: 18-22 minutes
With music, entrance, and exit: 27-35 minutes

Interfaith Ceremony

WELCOME

We have gathered together in this place to witness and experience one of life's most precious moments. (Groom's full name) _____ and (Bride's full name) _____ have invited us to share in the celebration of their love as they commit themselves to each other in marriage. Every marriage ceremony is unique, and today, not only are two special people being joined together, but two faiths, as well. Out of two different and distinct traditions, they have come together to learn the best of what each has to offer, appreciating their differences, and confirming that being together is far better than being apart from each other. As we bless this marriage under a huppah, the Jewish symbol of the new home being created here, we will later light the Unity Candle, a Christian symbol of two people becoming one in marriage. May your life together be a witness to others that people can live together in peace in spite of differences. Your marriage then becomes a sign, a very precious sign, that nothing is stronger than love. The Bible says, *"Love bears all things, believes all things, hopes all things, endures all things. Love never fails. So faith, hope, and love abide, these three; but the greatest of these is love."*

CONSENT

So I now ask you, (Groom) _____, is it your desire to marry this woman who is your beloved, your friend, and whose heart you possess?

(The Groom shall say): **Yes, it is my desire.**

And (Bride) _____, is it your desire to marry this man who is your beloved, your friend, and whose heart you possess?

(The Bride shall say): **Yes, it is my desire.**

Who presents (Bride) _____ to be married to (Groom) _____?

(The Escort/Parents shall say): **Her Mother and I** or **I do** or **We do** or **Her family** or other.

(The Escort/Parents may either be seated or remain at the altar with the Bridal Party.)

(Bride gives bouquet to Maid of Honor.)

ADDRESS AND READINGS

Marriage is a supreme sharing of experiences, an adventure in the most intimate of human relationships. It is the union of two people whose friendship has grown and matured to the place where they now desire to share life together as one. I wish to say to all of you here today that the future of (Groom's) _____ and (Bride's) _____ home together depends also upon you. It is through your thoughts, your feelings, and your acts that you can help strengthen their bond. For you see, marriage does not thrive in isolation, but rather in the fellowship of family and friends. (Groom) _____ and (Bride) _____ welcome the wisdom and strength of their family and friends to help their love grow, for it is through this love that they themselves have grown.

(Groom) _____ and (Bride) _____, you symbolize a lesson in love and harmony, encouraging all of us to seek a common bond. You come before us with a spirit of human unity, a high regard for the institution of marriage, a strong love for each other, family, and friends, and a faith in God common to each of your individual upbringing. You have chosen to focus on your similarities rather than your differences. You have learned to respect the other's heritage by celebrating their traditions along with yours. I know each of you considers your religious beliefs and traditions to be precious. In marriage, you are not sacrificing your commitment to these things, but rather reaffirming them and promising to share what is the best of both traditions with one another. One of those traditions is the blessing of this marriage under a huppah or canopy. Let me explain the significance of this custom.

Explanation of the Huppah:

Long after the tents vanished from the Jewish landscape, wedding ceremonies were held out of doors in hope that the marriage would be blessed with as many children as there were "stars of the heavens." In order to create a more modest and sanctified space, a kind of covering was designed—hence, the huppah. As you can see, the huppah is open on all four sides out of respect for Abraham, who had doors on all four sides of his home so that visitors would always know they were welcome.

The huppah does not promise that love, hope, or even pledges to one another will keep out the elements, or adversity, or even heartache. In fact, the flimsiness of the huppah is a reminder that the only thing that really makes a house a home is the people in it who love each other and choose to be together—to be a family. The only anchor they have will be holding onto God and holding onto each other. The huppah, therefore, symbolizes a place where the lives of these two people are woven together and intertwined with God's love, so that they truly become one in every way. Let me share with you a reading that best describes this relationship.

Weave My Love Into Yours

To be married is to enter a new realm of life.
You have left behind the room of childhood and now have stepped over the threshold
    into the room of adult love and commitment.
It is within the bonds of this commitment that two distinctly different personalities
    are blended into one...this process takes years.
It is like the weaving together of two distinctly different kinds of thread
    into a whole new cloth...a cloth with many functions.
It is a tent...
    a covering from the hostile elements of the changing seasons.
It is a colorful quilt...
    that warms the two who share it.
It is a sheer, gauzy curtain...
    that offers privacy while allowing the sunlight to shine through.
But the most beautiful and enduring marriage of all
    is not merely the weaving of two lives, but of three,
For woven into the strongest unions
    is the golden strand of God's love that endures forever.
May the cloth of your marriage be woven of three strands,
    For "...a threefold cord is not easily broken." *Ecclesiastes 4:12*
                            (Reading #6)

WEDDING VOWS

(The Officiant shall say): (Groom)_____, please repeat after me.

(Bride) _____, I thank God for bringing you into my life. / I choose you this day / as my wife, my love, and my best friend. / I commit myself to you / openly, exclusively, and eternally. / I promise you my unconditional love, / I give you my unwavering trust, / and I share with you all the days of my life. *(Wedding Vow #3a)*

(The Officiant shall say): (Bride)_____, please repeat after me.

(Groom) _____, I accept you / as the one God has chosen to complete me. / I join with you now / to share all that life may bring. / I will be yours / through weakness and strength, / through sorrow and joy, / through failure and triumph. / I give my love to you and you alone / with all my heart, soul, and mind / now, forever, and always. *(Wedding Vow #3b)*

EXPLANATION OF THE RINGS

The wedding ring is a symbol of the unbroken circle of love, for love freely given has no beginning and no end. Once these rings are given and received, they seal the covenant that you have made with one another. May these rings always be a loving reminder of the ties that bind you together forever as husband and wife.

RING EXCHANGE VOWS

(The Officiant shall say):
May I have the tokens of (Groom's) _____ and (Bride's) _____ love for each other?

(The Officiant receives the rings from Best Man and Maid of Honor.)

(The Officiant shall then say): Bless these rings, O Lord, that those who wear them, who give and receive them, may be ever faithful to one another, remain in Your peace, and live and grow old together in Your love. Amen.

(Groom places ring on Bride's finger.)

(The Officiant shall say): (Groom) _____, please repeat after me.

(Bride) _____, with this ring, I marry you. / You are now my wife, / my beloved, / my friend. / Where you go, I will go, / and where you live, I will live. / Your people will be my people, / and your God, my God. *(Ring Vow #12, Version 2*)*

(Bride places ring on Groom's finger.)

(The Officiant shall say): (Bride) _____, please repeat after me.

(Groom) _____, with this ring, I marry you. / You are now my husband, / my beloved, / my friend. / Where you go, I will go, / and where you live, I will live. / Your people will be my people, / and your God, my God. *(Ring Vow #12, Version 2*)*

*Ring Vow #12, Version 1 may be used instead.

LIGHTING OF THE UNITY CANDLE
(Or Other Optional Wedding Tradition)

(Groom) _____ and (Bride) _____ have chosen to light the Unity Candle, a symbol of Christian love and unity. Today, it also symbolizes the joining together of two hearts, two homes, and two heritages into one. It is written, *"For this cause shall a man leave his father and mother, and shall cleave to his wife, and the two shall become one flesh."* Three candles stand before you. The two outer candles represent the lives of (Groom) _____ and (Bride) _____ and their families who nurtured them in their beliefs. Until now, both have let their light shine as individuals in their respective homes and communities. Today, as they light the center candle, they join their lights and their love in this new union as husband and wife. They do not lose their individuality, yet in marriage, they are united in so close a bond that they truly do become one in heart, mind, and soul. A famous rabbi once wrote: "From every human being there rises a light that reaches straight to heaven. And when two souls are destined to find one another, their two streams of light flow together, and a single brighter light goes forth from their united being." It is our prayer that you will continually rekindle the candles of your love throughout your lives, so that there always will be light and joy, peace and harmony in your hearts and in your home.

THE UNITY CUP
(Kiddush Cup)

(Two separate goblets are filled with wine. The Officiant pours one-half the wine from each goblet into a separate cup, the Unity Cup, from which the Bride and Groom each sips after the Officiant explains its meaning.)

(The Officiant shall say): This glass of wine is known as the Unity Cup, or Kiddush Cup, and is symbolic of the Cup of Life. As you share this cup of wine, you share all that the future may bring. The half-filled goblets are a reminder of your individuality; the single cup marks your new life together. As you share the wine from a single cup, so may you, under God's guidance, share contentment, peace, and fulfillment from your own Cup of Life. May you find life's joys heightened, its bitterness sweetened, and each of its moments hallowed by true companionship and love.

(The Officiant holds up the Unity Cup and may then say this prayer): Blessed art Thou, O Lord our God, Creator of the fruit of the vine.

(The Groom takes a sip of wine first, then offers the cup to the Bride.)

WEDDING PRAYER/BLESSING

(The Officiant shall say): I would like to bless your marriage with this old Irish blessing:
May the road rise to meet you. May the wind be always at your back. May the sun shine warm upon your face, the rains fall soft upon the fields. May the light of friendship guide your paths together. May the laughter of children grace the halls of your home. May the joy of living for one another trip a smile from your lips, a twinkle from your eye. And when eternity beckons at the end of a life heaped high with love, may the good Lord embrace you with the arms that have nurtured you the whole length of your joy-filled days. May the gracious God hold you both in the palm of His hands. And today, may the Spirit of Love find a dwelling place in your hearts. Amen. *(Blessing #12)*

THE PRONOUNCEMENT

(Groom) _____ and (Bride) _____, as you stand before God, and with the support of your family and friends, you have declared your commitment to each other. You have expressed your desire to be one by sharing the Unity Cup and lighting the Unity Candle. You have spoken your vows of love and have given and received these rings to forever symbolize your faithfulness to one another. Therefore, with God's blessing, it is with great joy that I now pronounce you husband and wife.

BREAKING OF THE GLASS

We conclude this ceremony with the Breaking of the Glass. In Jewish tradition, the Breaking of the Glass at a wedding is a symbolic prayer and hope that your love for one another will remain until the pieces of the glass come together again, or in other words, that your love will last forever. The fragile nature of the glass also suggests the frailty of human relationships. Even the strongest of relationships is subject to disintegration. The glass then, is broken to "protect" the marriage with this prayer: May your bond of love be as difficult to break as it would be to put the pieces of this glass together again.

(The Officiant, directing his attention to the guests, then says): After the groom breaks the glass, I invite everyone to shout "Mazel Tov!" which means "Good luck and Congratulations!"

(The Officiant or Best Man places the glass on the floor next to the Groom. The Groom breaks the glass with his foot and everyone shouts "Mazel Tov!")

KISS

(The Officiant shall say): (Groom) _____, you may kiss your Bride.

(Bride and Groom kiss.)

(Bride receives bouquet from Maid of Honor.)

PRESENTATION

(The Officiant shall say): Ladies and Gentlemen, it is my privilege to introduce to you for the very first time, (Mr. and Mrs.) _____.

Bilingual Traditional Ceremony

(English–Spanish / Inglés–Español)

Approximate Time: 15-25 minutes
With music, entrance, and exit: 25-35 minutes

El Tiempo Aproximado: 15-25 minutos
Con la música, la entrada, y la salida: 25-35 minutos

TRADITIONAL CEREMONY
(English)

WELCOME

We welcome all of you here today as we have come together in the presence of God and these witnesses to join (Groom) _____ and (Bride) _____ in holy matrimony. Marriage is a gift, a gift from God, given to us so that we might experience the joys of unconditional love with a life-long partner.

CONSENT

(Groom)_____, do you take (Bride) _____ to be your wedded wife, to live together after God's ordinance in the holy estate of matrimony? Do you promise to love her, comfort her, respect her, honor and keep her, in sickness and in health, in prosperity and adversity, and forsaking all others, remain faithful to her as long as you both shall live?

(The Groom shall say): **I do.**

(Bride) _____, do you take (Groom) _____ to be your wedded husband, to live together after God's ordinance in the holy estate of matrimony? Do you promise to love him, comfort him, respect him, honor and keep him, in sickness and in health, in prosperity and adversity, and forsaking all others, remain faithful to him as long as you both shall live?

(The Bride shall say): **I do.**

Who gives (Bride) _____ to be married to (Groom)_____?

(The Escort shall say): **Her parents** or **Her Mother and her Father** or **Her family** or **I do.**

(Bride gives bouquet to Maid of Honor.)

LA CEREMONIA TRADICIONAL
(Español)

LA BIENVENIDA

Les damos la más cordial bienvenida al hoy reunirnos en la presencia de Dios y estos testigos para unir a (el Novio) _____ y (la Novia) _____ en sagrado matrimonio. El matrimonio es un regalo, un regalo de Dios, dado a nosotros para que podamos vivir la felicidad de un amor incondicional con un compañero de vida.

EL ACUERDO

(el Novio) _____, ¿acepta a (la Novia) _____ como su esposa, para vivir unidos conforme a lo ordenado por Dios, en el estado del santo matrimonio? ¿Promete amarla, consolarla, respetarla, honrarla y cuidarla, en enfermedad y en salud, en prosperidad y en adversidad, rechazando a todas las demás, y mantenenerse fiel a ella mientras vivan los dos?

(El Novio contestará diciendo): **Sí, acepto.**

(la Novia) _____, ¿acepta a (el Novio) _____ como su esposo, para vivir unidos conforme a lo ordenado por Dios, en el estado del santo matrimonio? ¿Promete amarlo, consolarlo, respetarlo, honrarlo y cuidarlo, en enfermedad y en salud, en prosperidad y en adversidad, rechazando a todos los demás, y mantenerse fiel a él mientras vivan los dos?

(La Novia contestará diciendo): **Sí, acepto.**

¿Quién entrega a (la Novia) _____ para que se case con (el Novio) _____?

(El Acompañante dirá): **Sus padres** o **Su Madre y su Padre** o **Su familia** o **Yo la entrego.**

(La Novia le da el ramo de flores a la Madrina de Honor.)

ADDRESS AND READINGS

(Groom)_____ and (Bride)_____, today is the beginning of a new life together for you. It marks the commencement of new relationships to your families, your friends, and to each other. I want both of you to know that God knew your needs when He brought you together. He knew exactly what you needed to make you complete. And now, God wants you to commit yourselves to accept each other as the one who completes you.

(Groom)_____, God's Word tells us what kind of a husband a man should be.

> *"And you husbands, show the same kind of love to your wives as Christ showed to the church when He died for her. That is how husbands should be toward their wives, loving them in the same kind of way." (Reading #11a)*

(Bride)_____, the qualities that make a woman truly beautiful have been written in the Holy Scriptures, the book of Proverbs:

> *"If you can find a truly good wife, she is worth more than precious gems! Her husband can trust her, and she will richly satisfy his needs. He praises her with these words: 'there are many fine women in the world, but you are the best of them all!'" (Reading #11b)*

In the Holy Bible, there is a chapter commonly known as the "Love Chapter"—I Corinthians, chapter 13.

> *"Love is patient and kind; love is not jealous or boastful; it is not arrogant or rude. Love does not insist on its own way; it is not irritable or resentful; it does not rejoice at wrong, but rejoices in the right. Love bears all things, believes all things, hopes all things, endures all things. Love never fails. So faith, hope, and love abide, these three; but the greatest of these is love."*
> *(Reading #12)*

LAS LECTURAS

(el Novio)_____ y (la Novia) _____, hoy es el principio de una nueva vida para ustedes. Marca el comienzo de una nueva relación con sus familias, sus amigos, y ustedes dos. Dios sabía sus necesidades cuando Él los unió. Quiero que los dos sepan que Él sabía exactamente lo que necesitaban ustedes para complementarse. Y ahora, Dios quiere que se hagan el compromiso de complementarse el uno al otro como a sí mismo.

(el Novio) _____, la palabra de Dios nos dice que clase de marido debe de ser el hombre.

> *"Y ustedes maridos, deben mostrar el mismo amor hacia sus mujeres así como Dios mostró a la iglesia cuando murió por ella. De esta manera los maridos deben ser hacia sus mujeres, amándolas de la misma manera." (Lectura #11a)*

(la Novia) _____, las cualidades que hacen a una mujer verdaderamente hermosa han sido escritas en los Proverbios de la Sagrada Escritura.

> *"¡Si puede encontrar una mujer virtuosa, ella es mas valiosa que las joyas! Su marido le puede confiar, y ella ampliamente satisface sus deseos. Él la elojía con estas palabras: '¡Hay muchas mujeres buenas en el mundo, pero tu eres la mejor de todas!'" (Lectura #11b)*

En la Santa Biblia, hay un capítulo que es bien conocido como "el Capítulo del Amor"—I Corintios, capítulo 13.

> *"El amor es paciente y bondadoso; en el amor no hay celos ni jactancias; no es arrogante o cruel; el amor no insiste en su propia manera; no es irritable o resentido; no se alegra de lo malo sino se alegra de lo bueno. El amor tolera todo, cree en todo, desea todo, sobrevive todo. El amor nunca falla. Así pues, permanecen la fe, la esperanza, y el amor, estos tres; pero el mayor de ellos es el amor." (Lectura #12)*

And so, (Groom) _____, if you will love (Bride) _____ as Christ loves the church, and (Bride) _____, if you will respond to (Groom) _____ as unto the Lord, your companionship as husband and wife will blossom into a physical, emotional, and spiritual closeness beyond which nothing can compare.

WEDDING VOWS

(The Officiant shall say): (Groom) _____, please repeat after me.

I, (Groom) _____, / take thee, (Bride) _____, / to be my wedded wife, / to have and to hold / from this day forward, / for better, for worse, / for richer, for poorer, / in sickness and in health, / to love and to cherish, / till death do us part. / This is my solemn vow.

(The Officiant shall say): (Bride) _____, please repeat after me.

I, (Bride) _____, / take thee, (Groom) _____, / to be my wedded husband, / to have and to hold / from this day forward, / for better, for worse, / for richer, for poorer, / in sickness and in health, / to love and to cherish, / till death do us part. / This is my solemn vow.

EXPLANATION OF THE RINGS

The wedding ring serves as a symbol of the promises you have just spoken. It is the outward and visible sign of an inward and invisible love that binds your hearts together.

(The Officiant shall say): May I have the token of (Groom's) _____ and (Bride's) _____ love for each other?

(Officiant receives rings from Ring Bearer or Ring Sponsors or other.)

Y así, (el Novio) _____, si usted le amará a (la Novia) _____ como Dios ama a la iglesia, y (la Novia) _____, si usted le responderá a (el Novio) _____ como al Señor, su compañerismo como esposo y esposa florecerá en la intimidad física, emocional, y espiritual las cuales no tendrán comparación.

LAS PROMESAS MATRIMONIALES

(El Oficiante dice): (el Novio) _____, por favor, repita después de mí.

Yo, (el Novio) _____, te tomo a ti, (la Novia) _____, / como mi esposa, / para tenerte y sostenerte / de hoy en adelante, / para bien o para mal, / en riqueza o en pobreza, / en enfermedad o en salud, / para amarte y respetarte, / hasta que la muerte nos separe. / Esta es mi solemne promesa.

(El Oficiante dice): (la Novia) _____, por favor, repita después de mí.

Yo, (la Novia) _____, te tomo a ti, (el Novio) _____, / como mi esposo, / para tenerte y sostenerte / de hoy en adelante, / para bien o para mal, / en riqueza o en pobreza, / en enfermedad o en salud, / para amarte y respetarte, / hasta que la muerte nos separe. / Esta es mi solemne promesa.

LA EXPLICACIÓN DE LOS ANILLOS

El anillo matrimonial sirve como un símbolo de las promesas que hoy se acaban de hacer. Es la señal exterior y visible del amor interno e invisible que une sus corazones.

(El Oficiante dice): ¿Me permiten los símbolos del amor de los novios, (el Novio) _____ y (la Novia) _____?

(El Oficiante recibe los anillos del Paje de Anillos o los Padrinos de Anillos u otro.)

BLESSING OF THE RINGS

Dear Lord, bless these rings that (Groom) _____ and (Bride) _____ give today. May these rings always be a symbol of their faithfulness, a seal upon their vows, and a reminder of their love. Amen.

RING EXCHANGE VOWS

(The Officiant shall say): (Groom) _____, please repeat after me.

With this ring, I thee wed, / and from this day forward, / I consecrate and commit / my love and my life / to you alone.

(The Officiant shall say): (Bride) _____, please repeat after me.

With this ring, I thee wed, / and from this day forward, / I consecrate and commit / my love and my life / to you alone.

THE UNITY CANDLE

The Unity Candle is a symbol of the union that exists between a man and a woman who enter the holy estate of matrimony. They are no longer two, but one. The Holy Bible says, *"For this cause shall a man leave his father and mother, and shall cleave to his wife, and they shall become one flesh."*

BLESSING OF THE HOLY BIBLE

(The Sponsors bring the Holy Bible and the Rosary and place them in the hands of the Bride and Groom.)

Lord, bless this Bible and the lives of those who read it. We know the Holy Bible is the Word of God. We pray that it may be the spiritual guide that lights your pathway and guides you in all your decisions so that your will and the will of God are one and the same. Amen.

(The Sponsors take the Holy Bible and the Rosary and sit down.)

LA BENDICIÓN DE LOS ANILLOS

Señor, bendice estos anillos que hoy se entregan (el Novio) _____ y (la Novia) _____ . Que estos anillos siempre sean un símbolo de su fidelidad, un sello de su promesa, y un recuerdo de su amor. Amén.

EL INTERCAMBIO DE LOS ANILLOS

(El Oficiante dice): (el Novio) _____, por favor, repita después de mí.

Con este anillo me caso contigo, / y de hoy en adelante, / consagro y comprometo / mi amor y mi vida / solamente a ti.

(El Oficiante dice): (la Novia) _____, por favor, repita después de mí.

Con este anillo me caso contigo, / y de hoy en adelante, / consagro y comprometo / mi amor y mi vida / solamente a ti.

LA VELA DE LA UNIDAD

La Vela de la Unidad es el símbolo de la unión que existe entre un hombre y una mujer que entran al terreno sagrado del santo matrimonio. Ya no son dos, sino uno solo. La Santa Biblia dice, *"Por tanto, dejará el hombre a su padre y a su madre, y se unirá a su mujer, y serán una sola carne."*

LA BENDICIÓN DE LA SANTA BIBLIA

(Los Padrinos traen la Santa Biblia y el Rosario y los ponen en las manos de los Novios.)

Señor, bendice esta Biblia y las vidas de los que la leen. Sabemos que la Santa Biblia es la Palabra de Dios. Pedimos que sea la guía espiritual que ilumine su sendero y les instruya en todas sus decisiones para que su voluntad y la voluntad de Dios sean la misma. Amén.

(Los Padrinos toman la Santa Biblia y el Rosario y se sientan.)

EXPLANATION OF THE COINS

(The Sponsors bring the box of coins and empty it into the Groom's hands.)

These thirteen coins are a symbol of the care that (Groom) _____ and (Bride) _____ will give in order that their home will have everything it needs. These coins also are a sign of the blessings of God and all the good things they will share together.

BLESSING OF THE COINS

Lord, bless these coins as a symbol of mutual help throughout their lives. Provide them with all they need for their home. We give you thanks for all the good things they are going to share because of Your many blessings, Lord. Amen.

COIN VOWS

(Groom drops the coins into the Bride's hands and says):
(Bride) _____, receive these thirteen coins / as a symbol of my dedication / in caring for our home / and providing for our family's necessities.

(Bride receives the coins from the Groom and says):
(Groom) _____, I accept your gift of dedication, / and I promise on my part / that everything provided / will be used with care / for the benefit of our home and family.

(The Sponsors take the coins and sit down.)

BLESSING OF THE LASSO

(The Sponsors bring forth the lasso and place it around the shoulders of the Bride and Groom.)

(Groom) _____ and (Bride) _____, this lasso represents the union of two hearts into one heart, two souls into one soul, and two lives into one life. (The Blessing) Oh Lord, bless this couple as they journey through life together. Unite them into one spirit . . . hand in hand, heart to heart, flesh to flesh, and soul to soul. Amen.

LA EXPLICACIÓN DE LAS ARRAS

(Los Padrinos traen la caja de arras y la vacían en las manos del Novio.)

Estas trece arras son el símbolo del cuidado que (el Novio) _____ y (la Novia) _____ tendrán para que su hogar tenga todo lo que necesite. Estas arras también son un signo de las bendiciones de Dios y de todos los bienes que compartirán juntos.

LA BENDICIÓN DE LAS ARRAS

Señor, bendice estas arras como un símbolo de la ayuda mutua que se darán en sus vidas. Proporcionales todo lo necesario para su hogar. Te agradecemos por todos los bienes que compartirán, gracias a tus bendiciones, Señor. Amén.

LAS PROMESAS DE LAS ARRAS

(El Novio pone las arras en las manos de la Novia y dice):
(la Novia) _____, recibe estas trece arras / como una prenda de mi dedicación / la cual cuidará de nuestro hogar / y proveerá de las necesidades de nuestra familia.

(La Novia recibe las arras del Novio y dice):
(el Novio) _____, yo acepto tu regalo de dedicación, / y te prometo de mi parte / que todo lo proveído / será usado con cuidado / para el beneficio de nuestro hogar y familia.

(Los Padrinos toman las arras y se sientan.)

LA BENDICIÓN DEL LAZO

(Los Padrinos traen el lazo y lo ponen alrededor de los hombros de los Novios.)

(el Novio) _____ y (la Novia) _____, este lazo representa la unión de dos corazones en uno solo, dos almas en una sola, y dos vidas en una sola. (La Bendición) O Dios, bendice a esta pareja ahora que emprenden el camino de la vida juntos. Únelos en un solo espíritu . . . mano con mano, corazón con corazón, carne con carne, y alma con alma. Amén.

WEDDING PRAYER / BLESSING

Our Heavenly Father, we ask Your blessing upon these two lives and the home they are establishing today. May the love they have for each other grow deeper and stronger because of their love for You. Lord, You guided them to each other, now guide them in this new journey as husband and wife. As they walk down this path, light their way so that they may keep their eyes focused on Your will, their hands holding fast to Your truth, their feet firmly planted in Your Word, and their hearts bound together by Your love. This we pray in the name of the Father, the Son, and the Holy Spirit. Amen.

(The Sponsors remove the lasso and sit down.)

PRONOUNCEMENT

(Groom)_____ and (Bride)_____, since you have consented together in holy matrimony and have pledged yourselves to each other by your solemn vows, by the giving of rings, and have declared your commitment of love before God and these witnesses, I now pronounce you husband and wife, in the name of the Father, the Son, and the Holy Spirit. Those whom God hath joined together, let no man separate.

KISS

(The Officiant shall say): (Groom)_____, you may kiss your Bride.

(Bride and Groom kiss.)

(Bride receives bouquet from Maid of Honor.)

PRESENTATION

(The Officiant shall say): Ladies and Gentlemen, it is an honor to introduce to you for the very first time: (Mr. and Mrs.)_____.

LA BENDICIÓN MATRIMONIAL

Padre nuestro, te pedimos tu bendición sobre estas dos vidas y el hogar que hoy inician juntos. Que el amor que se tienen el uno al otro crezca más grande y más fuerte gracias al amor que sienten hacia ti. Señor, tu los guiaste el uno al otro, ahora guíalos en esta nueva jornada como esposos. A medida que pasen por este camino, ilumina su sendero para que puedan mantener sus ojos enfocados hacia ti y tu voluntad, sus manos agarradas a tu verdad, sus pies plantados firmemente en tu palabra, y sus corazones unidos por tu amor. Oramos en el nombre del Padre, del Hijo, y del Espíritu Santo. Amén.

(Los Padrinos se quitan el lazo y se sientan.)

LA DECLARACIÓN

(el Novio) _____ y (la Novia) _____, ya que han consentido ingresar en santo matrimonio, y que han prometido el uno al otro votos solemnes, por medio de la entrega de anillos, y ya que han declarado su promesa de amor ante Dios y estos testigos, ahora yo los declaro marido y mujer (esposo y esposa), en el nombre del Padre, del Hijo, y del Espíritu Santo. Por tanto, lo que Dios ha unido, que no lo separe el hombre.

EL BESO

(El Oficiante dice): (el Novio) _____, puede besar a la Novia.

(Los Novios se besan.)

(La Novia recibe el ramo de flores de la Madrina de Honor.)

LA PRESENTACIÓN

(El Oficiante dice): Damas y Caballeros, es un honor presentarles por primera vez a:
(el Señor y la Señora) _____.

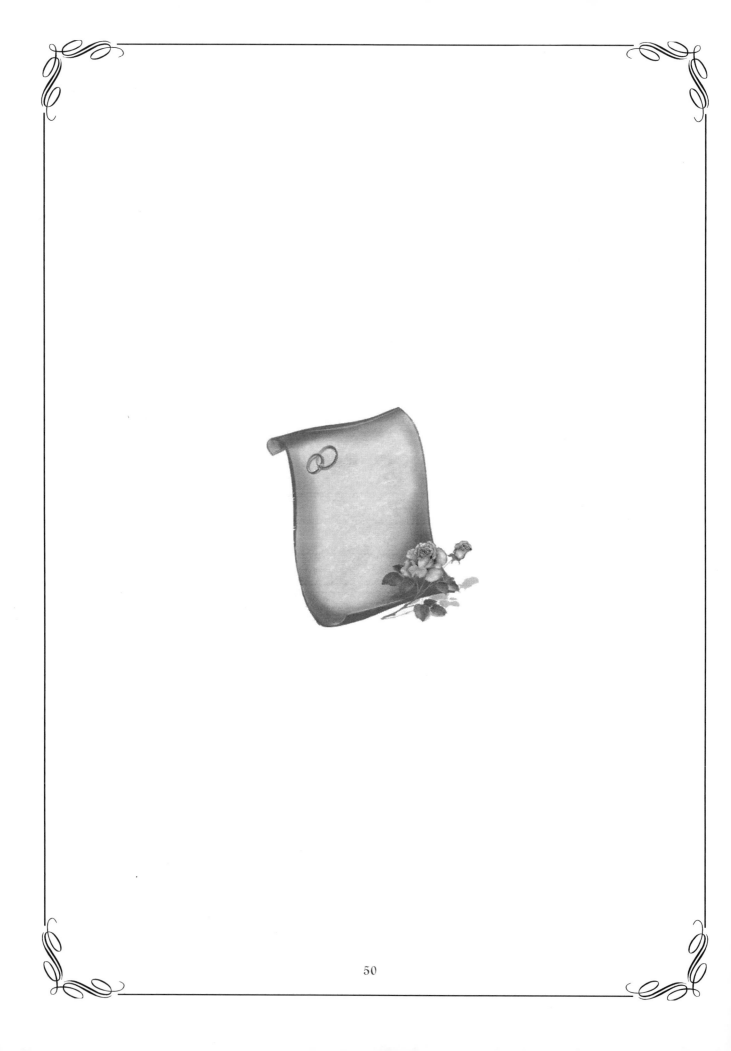

Vow Renewal Ceremony

(For Celebrating Recommitments)

Approximate Time: 12-15 minutes
With music, entrance, and exit: 20-25 minutes

Vow Renewal Ceremony

WELCOME

Friends and family of (Husband) _____ and (Wife) _____, today, we have come together to bear witness to the fact that real love, true love, is something so pure and so powerful that it can endure the challenges of life and withstand the tests of time. (Husband) _____ and (Wife) _____, _____ years ago, you took your wedding vows, and though many things have changed in your lives since then, one thing has remained constant—your love. When the two of you got married, you promised to be faithful to each other in good times and bad; you promised to be true to each other whether you were rich or poor; you promised to love each other in sickness and in health. You certainly have had your share of these times, but you have been faithful and true, and your love has grown and matured into the wonderful relationship we see today. Now you have come to recommit yourselves to each other and to those promises you made _____ years ago.

CONSENT

(Husband) _____ and (Wife) _____, is it your heart's desire to publicly recommit yourselves to each other in marriage and to renew your vows of faithfulness and love?

(Both answer): **Yes.**

I have one final question. After all you have been through together over the years, would you do it all over again?

(Both answer): **Yes, we would do it all over again.**

ADDRESS AND READINGS

What is it about this institution of marriage that would make us want to do it all over again? It may be true that marriages are made in heaven, but man is responsible for the maintenance. You two have made your marriage the most important thing on earth, and you have made each other the most important person in your life. When you were first married, you thought you knew what love was. But as you look back on all your years together, you realize now that your love at its beginning, although real and true, was only a shallow imitation of the love you have for each other today.

Through all the seasons of your life, you have grown deeper and deeper in love, and by God's grace, that love has matured into a precious and priceless companionship. There is no greater joy than to walk through this world with your one true companion, sharing all the experiences that life may hold. God has given you a lifetime of shared memories together—shared joys and shared sorrows. Cherish and treasure those memories, happy and sad, for they are the souvenirs of your hearts. And that is why "we would do it all over again."

If you could put into writing the journey of your love together over the past _____ years, what would you say? Where would you begin? How would you express your feelings on paper? Someone has penned the words to those sentiments in a heartfelt poem that I would like to share with you. I believe it expresses what you both feel in your hearts. The poem is entitled, "I'd Marry You Again."

I'd Marry You Again

With tiny tears that glistened,
　　　my eyes were fixed on you;
and thinking of the life we'd share,
　　　we softly said, "I do."
Our hearts were knit together
　　　from the time that we first met;
and memories were gathered
　　　that we never will forget.
While daily living life with you,
　　　you saw the real in me;
and still you chose acceptance,
　　　a loving mystery.
With many happy times gone by,
　　　and others when we cried;
some days we'd share so endlessly,
　　　while other days we'd hide.
With all the ups and downs we've had
　　　in learning to be friends;
I know that in this heart of mine
　　　I'd marry you again.

(Reading #8)

WEDDING VOWS

(Your original vows may be used here or you may personalize your own reaffirmation vows)

(Wife) _____, (Husband) _____ was once upon a time your "knight in shining armor." Well, your knight in shining armor is now your king, with dents and rust and squeaky joints. And (Husband) _____, (Wife) _____ was once your "fair young princess." And now your fair young princess is your queen, with a crown of curlers, cold cream, and crow's feet. But in spite of these little imperfections, your love still compels you to look past the surface and deeply into each other's heart. For what you see there is what brings you here—a love worth recommitting to "for as long as you both shall live."

(The Officiant shall say): At this time, (Husband) _____ and (Wife) _____ would like to share their vows of love and recommitment with each other.

(Wife / Husband) _____/_____, I love you. You have brought such joy to my life. Thank you for loving me as I am and taking me into your heart. I vow to return your love in full as we grow together as husband and wife. Through all the changes of our lives, I promise to be there for you always as a strength in need, a comfort in sorrow, a counselor in difficulty, and a companion in joy. This is my promise to you. *(Wedding Vow #4)*

NOTE: These wedding vows are best if read rather than repeated.

EXPLANATION OF THE RINGS

(First version — Using original rings)

When these rings were placed on your hands _____ years ago, they were shiny and new, perfect in form, without defect, and yet, untested. But now they have been worn day in and day out, through the ups and downs, the grit and grime, and the nuts and bolts of life, so that today these rings bear witness to a love that has substance, depth, quality, and most of all, endurance. The beauty of these rings is not in the glimmer or the sparkle. The real beauty lies in the nicks and the scratches and the wear and tear that makes these tokens of your love tested, tried, and true. May these rings always be a reminder of your commitment to "go the distance" with a love that lasts "until death do us part."

(Second version — Using new rings)

First came the engagement ring, the promise of your future together. Then came the wedding band when you vowed to love and cherish until the end of your days. Now comes this ring of renewal, celebrating your _____ years together as husband and wife, and reaffirming your commitment to each other for all the joyous years yet to come. Your past and your future are a circle unbroken, like this ring, symbolizing the memory of all your yesterdays and the hope for all your tomorrows.

RING EXCHANGE VOWS

(Original ring vows may be used here)

(The Officiant shall say): May I have the token of (Husband's) _____ love for (Wife)_____ ?

(Officiant receives ring from Best Man. Husband places ring on Wife's finger.)

(The Officiant shall then say): (Husband) _____, please repeat after me.

(Bride) _____, you are more precious to me today than yesterday, / and you will be more cherished tomorrow than you are today. / Please wear this ring / as a symbol of my eternal love for you, / a love that transcends all of our yesterdays, / all of our todays, / and all of our tomorrows. *(Ring Vow #6)*

(The Officiant shall say): May I have the token of (Wife's) _____ love for (Husband) _____?

(Officiant receives ring from Maid of Honor. Wife places ring on Husband's finger.)

(The Officiant shall then say): (Wife) _____, please repeat after me.

(Groom) _____, you are more precious to me today than yesterday, / and you will be more cherished tomorrow than you are today. / Please wear this ring / as a symbol of my eternal love for you, / a love that transcends all of our yesterdays, / all of our todays, / and all of our tomorrows. *(Ring Vow #6)*

NOTE: These ring vows are best if read rather than repeated.

LIGHTING OF THE UNITY CANDLE

The Unity Candle may signify many things, but today it symbolizes the coming together of your past and your future. When you were first married, the flames of your love burned brightly, but we all know that fire tends to die out if not tended to. And so, you must rekindle those flames every day if the light of your love is to endure. As you rekindle this Unity Candle today, may you continue to light up each other's life for as long as God gives you breath.

WEDDING PRAYER/BLESSING

May all that you are, always be in love; and may all that is love, always be in you. May your love be as beautiful on each day you share as it is on this day of celebration. And may each day you share be as precious to you as the day you first fell in love. May you always see and encourage the best in each other. May the challenges life brings your way make your marriage even stronger. And may you always be each other's best friend and greatest love.

(Blessing #6)

PRONOUNCEMENT

(Husband) _____ and (Wife) _____, as you stand before us after _____ years of marriage, we see a love that is pure, a love that is priceless, and a love that is permanent. Your example has renewed our faith in the strength of hope and the power of love. Because you have recommitted yourselves to each other and to this blessed institution we call marriage, I now bestow upon you once again, the most honorable titles of husband and wife.

KISS

(The Officiant shall say): (Groom) _____, you may kiss your Bride.

(Bride and Groom kiss.)

(Bride receives bouquet from Maid of Honor.)

PRESENTATION

(The Officiant shall say): Ladies and Gentlemen, it is my great pleasure to present to you for the second time, (Mr. and Mrs.) _____.

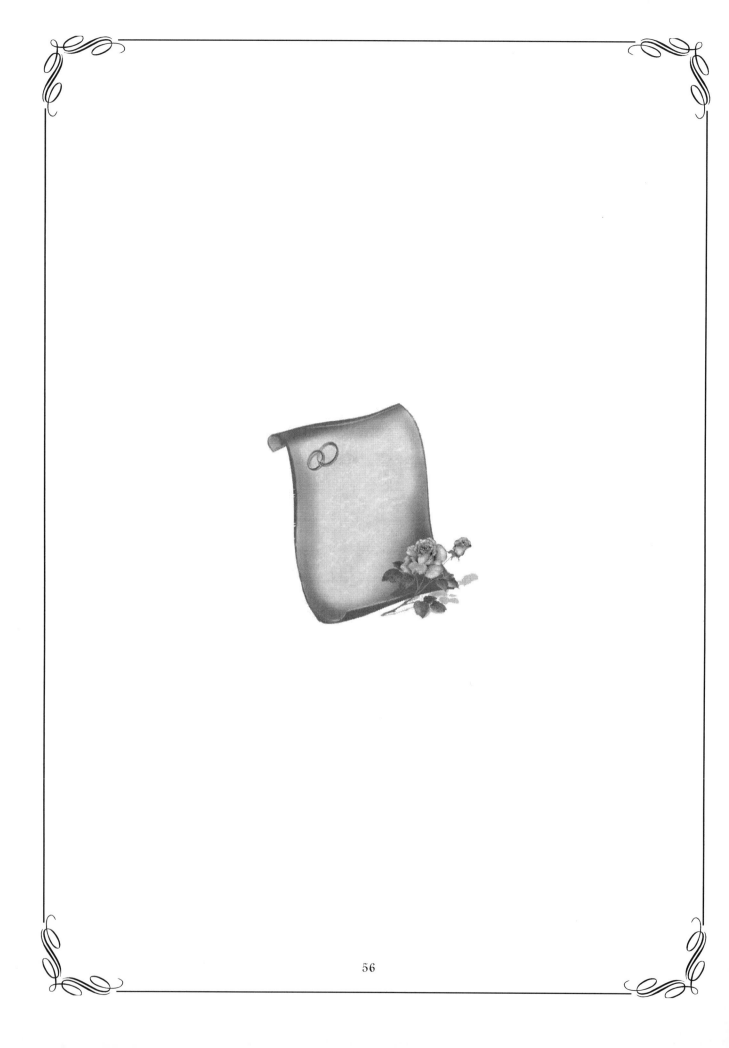

Readings

Love bears all things, believes all things,
hopes all things, endures all things.
Love never fails . . .

READINGS

1)

The Institution of Marriage

The institution of marriage was begun
    that a man and a woman
        might learn how to love
           and, in loving, know joy;
    that a man and a woman
        might learn how to share pain and loneliness
           and, in sharing, know strength;
    that a man and a woman
        might learn how to give
           and, in giving, know communion.

The institution of marriage was begun
    that a man and a woman
        might through their joy, their strength,
          and their communion,
             become creators of life itself.

Marriage is a high and holy state,
    to be held in honor
        among all men and women.
Marriage is a low and common state,
    to be built of the stuff
        of daily life.

Men and women are not angels, nor are they gods.
    Love can become hatred;
        joy, sorrow;
           marriage, divorce.

But human beings are not condemned to failure.
    Love can grow even in a real world.
        The wounds of sorrow can be healed,
          And new life built
            on the learnings of the old.

This is the reason for our gathering today:
    to renew our faith
        in the strength of hope
          and the power of love.

Kenneth W. Phifer

2) ## The Art of Marriage

The little things are the big things.
It is never being too old to hold hands.
It is remembering to say "I love you" at least once a day.
It is never going to sleep angry.
It is at no time taking the other for granted; the courtship should not end
    with the honeymoon, it should continue through all the years.
It is having a mutual sense of values and common objectives;
    it is facing the world together.
It is forming a circle of love that gathers in the whole family.
It is doing things for each other, not in the attitude of duty or sacrifice,
    but in the spirit of joy.
It is speaking words of appreciation and demonstrating gratitude in thoughtful ways.
It is not expecting the husband to wear a halo or the wife to have the wings of an angel.
It is not looking for perfection in each other.
It is cultivating flexibility, patience, understanding, and a sense of humor.
It is having the capacity to forgive and forget.
It is giving each other an atmosphere in which each can grow.
It is finding room for the things of the spirit.
It is the common search for the good and the beautiful.
It is the establishing of a relationship in which the independence is equal,
    the dependence is mutual, and the obligation is reciprocal.
And finally, it is not only marrying the right partner, it is being the right partner.

Wilferd A. Peterson

3) ## The Creation of Woman from the Rib of Man

The Lord God caused the man to fall into a deep sleep;
    and while he was sleeping, He took one of the man's ribs,
        and then closed up the place with flesh.
Then the Lord God formed a woman
    from the rib He had taken out of the man,
        and brought her to him.
The man said "This is now bone of my bones
    and flesh of my flesh;
        she shall be called Woman, for she was taken out of Man."

Genesis 2:21-23

Woman was made of a rib out of the side of Man.
    She was not created from Man's head to rule over him,
        nor from his feet to be trampled upon by him.
Instead, Woman was taken from his side to be equal with him;
    under his arm to be protected;
        and near his heart to be loved.

Matthew Henry

4)

When a Man and a Woman Are in Love

When a man and a woman are in love,
    his life lies within hers and her life lies within his.
Each lives as an individual,
    yet they also live for one another.
Each strives for independent goals,
    but they also work together to achieve their dreams.
When a man and a woman are in love,
    they will give to one another what they need to survive
    and help fulfill each other's wants.
They will turn one another's
    disappointment into satisfaction.
They will turn one another's
    frustration into contentment.
They will work as a mirror,
    reflecting to each other their strengths and weaknesses.
They will work together
    to alleviate the emotional walls that may separate them.
They will work together to build
    a better understanding of one another.
They will learn to lean on each other,
    but not so much as to be a burden on the other.
They will learn to reach out to one another,
    but not so much as to suffocate the other.
They will learn when it is time to speak
    and when it is time to listen.
They will be there to comfort each other
    in times of sorrow.
They will be there to celebrate together
    in times of happiness.
They will be one another's friend,
    guiding each other to the happiness that life holds.
They will be one another's companion,
    facing together the challenges that life may present.
When a man and a woman are in love,
    his life lies within hers and her life lies within his.
Together they will love one another
    for the rest of their lives
      and forever.

Stephen T. Fader

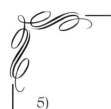

5)

Marriage Joins Two People in the Circle of Its Love

Marriage is a commitment to life, to the best that two people can find and bring out in each other. It offers opportunities for sharing and growth that no other human relationship can equal; a joining that is promised for a lifetime.

Within the circle of its love, marriage encompasses all of life's most important relationships. A wife and a husband are each other's best friend, confidant, lover, teacher, listener, and critic. There may come times when one partner is heartbroken or ailing, and the love of the other may resemble the tender caring of a parent for a child.

Marriage deepens and enriches every facet of life. Happiness is fuller; memories are fresher; commitment is stronger; even anger is felt more strongly, and passes away more quickly.

Marriage understands and forgives the mistakes life is unable to avoid. It encourages and nurtures new life, new experiences, and new ways of expressing love through the seasons of life.

When two people pledge to love and care for each other in marriage, they create a spirit unique to themselves, which binds them closer than any spoken or written words. Marriage is a promise, a potential, made in the hearts of two people who love, which takes a lifetime to fulfill.

Edmund O'Neill

6)

Weave My Love Into Yours

To be married is to enter a new realm of life.
You have left behind the room of childhood and now have stepped over the threshold
    into the room of adult love and commitment.
It is within the bonds of this commitment that two distinctly different personalities
    are blended into one…this process takes years.
It is like the weaving together of two distinctly different kinds of thread
    into a whole new cloth…a cloth with many functions.
It is a tent…
    a covering from the hostile elements of the changing seasons.
It is a colorful quilt…
    that warms the two who share it.
It is a sheer, gauzy curtain…
    that offers privacy while allowing the sunlight to shine through.
But the most beautiful and enduring marriage of all
    is not merely the weaving of two lives, but of three,
For woven into the strongest unions
    is the golden strand of God's love that endures forever.
May the cloth of your marriage be woven of three strands,
    For "…a threefold cord is not easily broken." *(Ecclesiastes 4:12)*

Claire Cloninger

7)

These Hands

These are the hands of your best friend, young and strong and full of love, that hold yours
   on your wedding day as you promise to love each other all the days of your life.
These are the hands that will work along side yours as you build your future together.
These are the hands that will passionately love you and care for you throughout the years.
These are the hands that will hold you when fear or grief fills your mind,
   and, with the slightest touch, will comfort you like no other.
These are the hands that will give you strength when you struggle,
   and support and encouragement to chase down your dreams.
These are the hands that will tenderly hold your children,
   and help keep your family together as one.
These are the hands that will, countless times, wipe the tears from your eyes,
   tears of sorrow and tears of joy.
And lastly, these are the hands that, even when wrinkled with age, will still be reaching for
   yours, still giving you the same unspoken tenderness with just a touch—
a touch from **These Hands.**

Author Unknown

Blessing of the Hands

(Optional—May be used with "These Hands" reading)

O God, bless these hands that are before You this day. May they always be held by one
another. Give them the strength to hold on during the storms of stress and the dark of
disillusionment. Keep them tender and gentle as they nurture each other in their wondrous
love. Help these hands to continue building a relationship founded in Your grace, rich in
caring for Your people, and devoted in reaching for Your perfection. And may you always
hold (Groom) _____ and (Bride) _____ in the palm of Your hand,
protecting them and guiding them in the way they should go. Amen.

8)

I'd Marry You Again

With tiny tears that glistened, my eyes were fixed on you;
   and thinking of the life we'd share, we softly said, "I do."
Our hearts were knit together from the time that we first met;
   and memories were gathered that we will never forget.
While daily living life with you, you saw the real in me;
   and still you chose acceptance, a loving mystery.
With many happy times gone by, and others when we cried;
   some days we'd share so endlessly, while other days we'd hide.
With all the ups and downs we've had in learning to be friends,
   I know that in this heart of mine I'd marry you again.

Anne Peterson

9)

Love

I love you not only for what you are,
　　but for what I am when I am with you.
I love you not only for what you have made of yourself,
　　but for what you are making of me.
I love you for the part of me that you brought out;
I love you for putting your hand into my heaped up heart
　　and passing over all the foolish, weak things
　　　　that you can't help dimly see there,
　　and for drawing out into the light all the beautiful belongings
　　　　that no one else had looked quite far enough to find.
I love you because you are helping me
　　to make of the lumber of my life not a tavern, but a temple,
　　out of the works of my everyday not a reproach, but a song.
You have done it without a touch, without a word.
You have done it by being yourself,
　　my companion and comforter, guide and friend,
　　　　the one I love.

Roy Croft

10)

Happy Home Recipe

Start with 1 heaping house full of Humans.

Add 1 cup each: Commitment, Cooperation, Courage, Courtesy, Consideration, and Contentment.

Allow 2 cups of open and honest Communication to simmer on low heat, but never let it come to a full boil.

Pour in 1 quart Milk of Human Kindness, along with 1 can Sweetened Condensed Confidence.

Add 3 tablespoons pure extract of "I Am Sorry,"
　　and mix well with a generous portion of Forgiveness, Patience, and Understanding.

Throw in a mouth full of Praise, Encouragement, and Support,
　　and season with a hand full of Loyalty and Friendship.

Stir in 1 big barrel of Laughter with just a pinch of Teasing,
　　and sprinkle with a pocket full of Hopes and Dreams.

Mix 1 gallon of Faith in God and Faith in each other with one heart full of Gratitude for countless blessings.

Continue to fill kettle until overflowing with Joy and Peace.

Carefully blend all the ingredients together into this big Pot of People and cook very slowly.

Remove any specks of Temper, Jealousy, or Criticism, and never serve with a Hot Tongue or a Cold Shoulder.

Sweeten well with a heapin' helpin' of Love and Tenderness,
　　and always keep warm with a steady flame of Devotion.

Remember to savor the flavor of every moment,
　　and if preserved with Care, this Happy Home will last a lifetime.

Carol Sage

Scripture Readings

Husbands

11a) And you husbands, show the same kind of love to your wives as Christ showed to the church when He died for her. That is how husbands should be toward their wives, loving them in the same kind of way. For since a man and his wife are now one, a man is really doing himself a favor and loving himself when he loves his wife! No one hates his own body but lovingly cares for it just as Christ cares for His body, the church, of which we are all parts. Husbands, live with your wives in an understanding way, giving them respect and treating them with honor since they are heirs together with you in the grace of life *(Ephesians 5:25, 28-30; 1 Peter 3:7).*

Wives

11b) If you can find a truly good wife, she is worth more than precious gems! Her husband can trust her, and she will richly satisfy his needs. She will not hinder him, but help him all her life. She is a woman of strength and dignity, and has no fear of old age. When she speaks, her words are wise, and kindness is the rule of everything she says. She watches carefully all that goes on throughout her household, and is never lazy. Her children stand and bless her; so does her husband. He praises her with these words, "There are many fine women in the world, but you are the best of them all!" Charm can be deceptive and beauty doesn't last, but a woman who fears and reverences God shall be greatly praised *(Proverbs 31:10-12, 25-29).*

The Love Chapter

12) Love is patient and kind; love is not jealous or boastful; it is not arrogant or rude. Love does not insist on its own way; it is not irritable or resentful; it does not rejoice at wrong, but rejoices in the right. Love bears all things, believes all things, hopes all things, endures all things. Love never fails. So faith, hope, and love abide, these three; but the greatest of these is love *(1 Corinthians 13:4-7,13) (Version 1–Traditional)*

Love is very patient and kind, never jealous or envious, never boastful or proud, never haughty or selfish or rude. Love does not demand its own way nor is it irritable or touchy. It does not hold grudges and will hardly ever notice when others do it wrong. It is never glad about injustice, but rejoices whenever truth wins out. This kind of love knows no boundaries to its tolerance, no end to its trust, no fading of its hope, no limit to its endurance. It can outlast anything. Love is, in fact, the one thing that still stands when all else has failed *(1 Corinthians 13:4-7,13) (Version 2–Contemporary)*

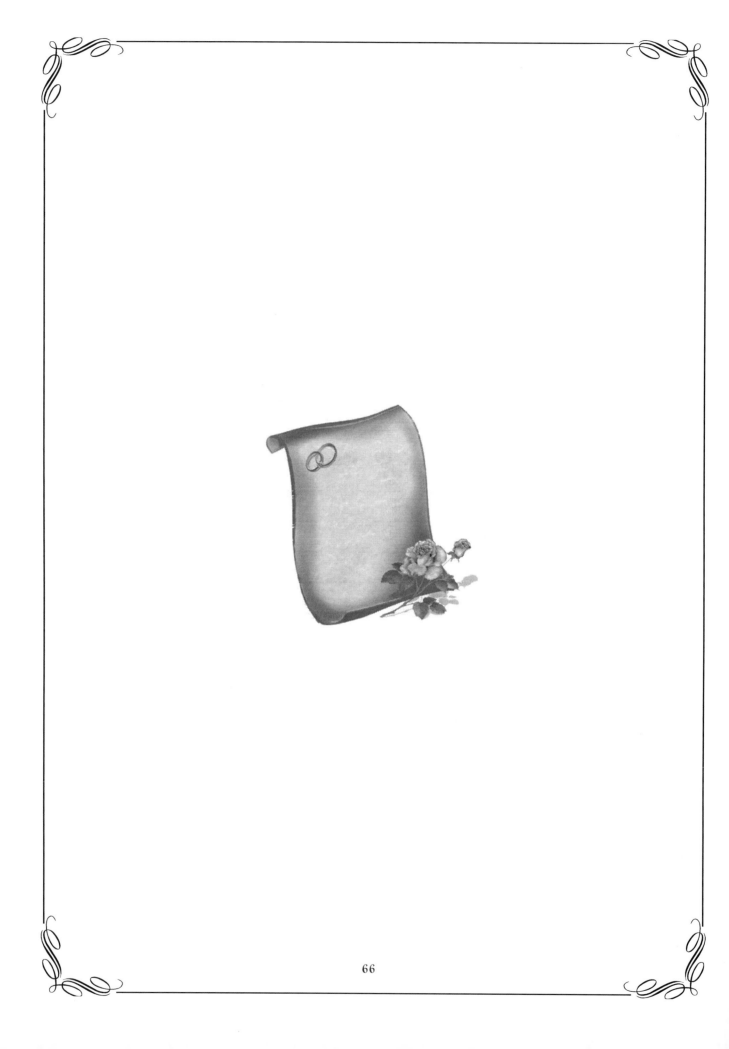

Wedding Vows

I promise to love, honor, and cherish you
as long as we both shall live . . .

Wedding Vows

1a) (Bride) _____, / I thank God He has given us to each other / to share one life, one love, one heart. / With God's help, / I will try to be everything / that He wants me to be for you, / so I may meet your needs / and fulfill your dreams. / I will love you with an unconditional love / just as Christ loves us. / In love I will lead you, / protect and provide for you, / nurture and care for you, / and honor and respect you. / I promise to stay by your side / no matter what circumstances life may bring, / and I vow to be faithful and true to you alone. / May my love give you strength all the days of our lives.

1b) (Groom) _____, / as we become husband and wife today, / I promise to love you with an unending love. / I give myself in all things to your care, / as unto the Lord. / As God has prepared me / to be your helpmate and companion in this life, / I commit myself to stand by you / whatever comes our way. / I will be with you in sickness and in health, / whether we are rich or poor, / and during times of happiness, / as well as times of sorrow. / I will honor and respect you, / encourage and support you, / and devote myself to you. / I promise to be faithful and true to you alone. / May my love bring you joy all the days of our lives.

2a) I, (Groom) _____, take you, (Bride) _____, / to be my partner in life. / I promise to walk by your side forever, / and to love, help, and encourage you / in all that you do. / I will take time to talk with you, / to listen to you, / and to care for you. / I will share your laughter and your tears / as your partner, lover, and best friend. / Everything I am and everything I have is yours / now and forevermore.

2b) I, (Bride) _____, give myself to you, (Groom) _____, / on this our wedding day. / I will cherish our friendship, / and love you today, tomorrow, and forever. / I will trust you and honor you. / I will love you faithfully / through the best and the worst, / through the difficult and the easy. / Whatever comes our way, I will be there always. / As I have given you my hand to hold, / so I give you my life to keep.

3a) (Bride) _____, I thank God for bringing you into my life. / I choose you this day / as my wife, my love, and my best friend. / I commit myself to you / openly, exclusively, and eternally. / I promise you my unconditional love, / I give you my unwavering trust, / and I share with you all the days of my life.

3b) (Groom) _____, I accept you / as the one God has chosen to complete me. / I join with you now / to share all that life may bring. / I will be yours / through weakness and strength, / through sorrow and joy, / through failure and triumph. / I give my love to you and you alone / with all my heart, soul, and mind / now, forever, and always.

4) (Bride/Groom) _____, I love you. You have brought such joy to my life. Thank you for loving me as I am and taking me into your heart. I vow to return your love in full as we grow together as husband and wife. Through all the changes of our lives, I promise to be there for you always as a strength in need, a comfort in sorrow, a counselor in difficulty, and a companion in joy. This is my promise to you. *(These wedding vows are best if read rather than repeated.)*

5) (Bride/Groom) _____, I accept you as my (wife/husband) and life companion / from this day forward. / I will share what I have and who I am. / I will be true to you in all things. / I will love you enough to risk being hurt, / and trust you when I misunderstand. / I will weep with you in heartache, / celebrate life with you in joy, / and cherish you as my partner / today, tomorrow, and always.

6) (Bride/Groom) _____, my promise to you is but a simple one. I will love you today and every day that follows until the end of time. With the passing of every minute, my love grows stronger and my devotion grows deeper. I will love and cherish you until my eyes can no longer see your gentle smile, my ears can no longer hear your loving words, and my hands can no longer feel your tender caress. From this moment until my dying breath, you are my love—you are my life. *(These wedding vows are best if read rather than repeated.)*

7) I, (Groom/Bride) _____ take you, (Bride/Groom) _____, / to be my partner in life. / I will cherish our friendship, / and love you today, tomorrow, and forever. / I will trust you and honor you. / I will love you faithfully / through the best and the worst, / through the difficult and the easy. / Whatever comes our way, I will be there always. / As I have given you my hand to hold, / so I give you my life to keep.

8) (Bride/Groom) _____, *(Option A)* God has given us a second chance at happiness. *(Option B)* We have been given a second chance at happiness. Before I met you, I was only half a person with an emptiness in my heart. But your love has filled that void completely, and I am whole again. Today is the first day of the rest of our lives. As we begin a new life together, I promise to give my future to you in faith, my heart to you in hope, and my life to you in love. *(These wedding vows are best if read rather than repeated.)*

9) I love you (Bride/Groom) _____, and I love (Children) _____ [as my very own]. Today, as we become husband and wife, we also will become a family and begin a new life together. I promise to be a faithful (husband/wife) and loving (father/mother), and I will be there for you and for the children always. No matter what circumstances life may bring, with God's help, we will face them together as a family. I commit myself to each of you from this day forward and forevermore. *(For marriages with children involved in the ceremony. These wedding vows are best if read rather than repeated.)*

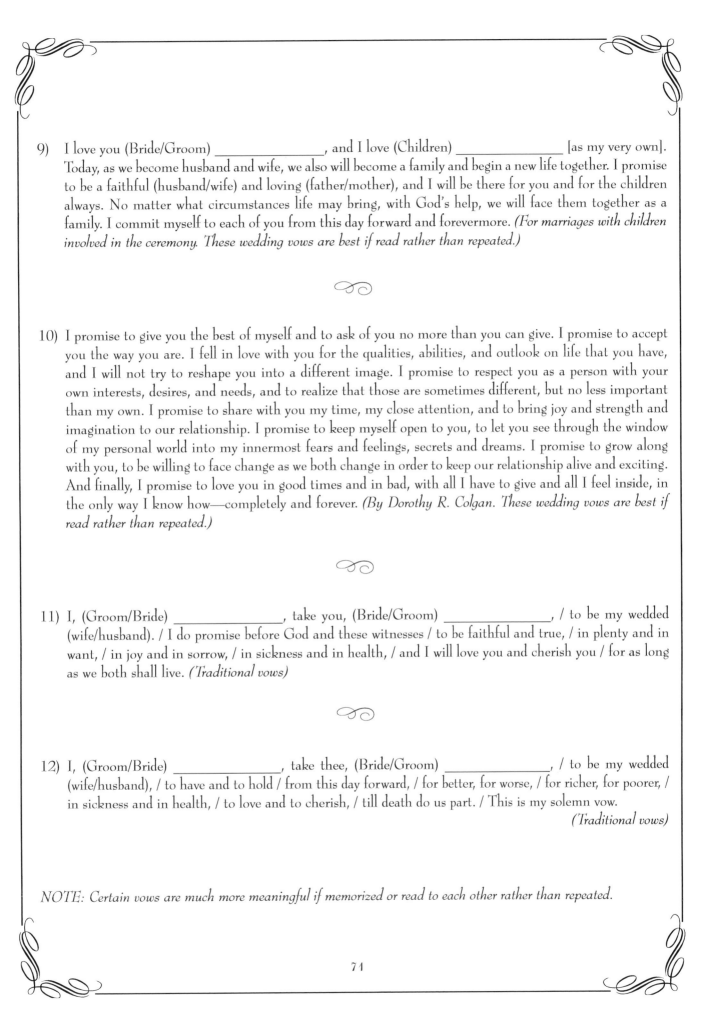

10) I promise to give you the best of myself and to ask of you no more than you can give. I promise to accept you the way you are. I fell in love with you for the qualities, abilities, and outlook on life that you have, and I will not try to reshape you into a different image. I promise to respect you as a person with your own interests, desires, and needs, and to realize that those are sometimes different, but no less important than my own. I promise to share with you my time, my close attention, and to bring joy and strength and imagination to our relationship. I promise to keep myself open to you, to let you see through the window of my personal world into my innermost fears and feelings, secrets and dreams. I promise to grow along with you, to be willing to face change as we both change in order to keep our relationship alive and exciting. And finally, I promise to love you in good times and in bad, with all I have to give and all I feel inside, in the only way I know how—completely and forever. *(By Dorothy R. Colgan. These wedding vows are best if read rather than repeated.)*

11) I, (Groom/Bride) _____, take you, (Bride/Groom) _____, / to be my wedded (wife/husband). / I do promise before God and these witnesses / to be faithful and true, / in plenty and in want, / in joy and in sorrow, / in sickness and in health, / and I will love you and cherish you / for as long as we both shall live. *(Traditional vows)*

12) I, (Groom/Bride) _____, take thee, (Bride/Groom) _____, / to be my wedded (wife/husband), / to have and to hold / from this day forward, / for better, for worse, / for richer, for poorer, / in sickness and in health, / to love and to cherish, / till death do us part. / This is my solemn vow.

(Traditional vows)

NOTE: Certain vows are much more meaningful if memorized or read to each other rather than repeated.

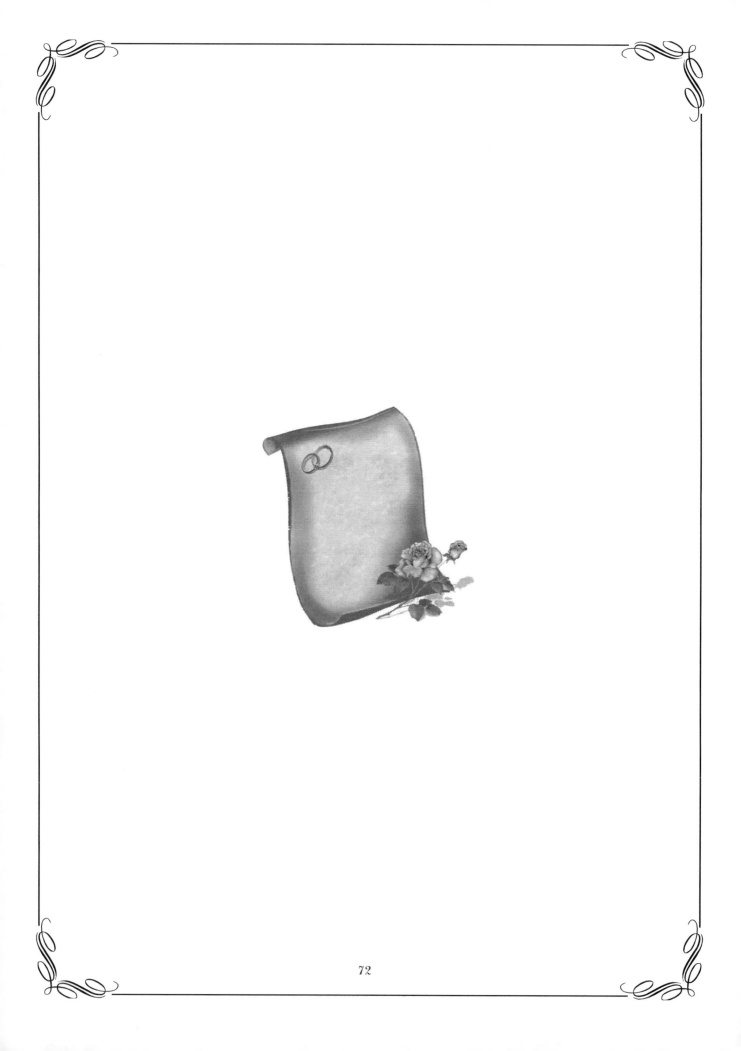

Ring Exchange Vows

With this ring, I thee wed . . .

Ring Exchange Vows

1a) (Bride/Groom) _____, this ring is a token of my love. / I marry you with this ring, / with all that I have and all that I am.

response

1b) (Groom/Bride) _____, I will forever wear this ring / as a sign of my commitment / and the desire of my heart.

❦

2) (Bride/Groom) _____, I give you this ring / as a symbol of my love and faithfulness, / and as I place it on your finger, / I commit my very heart and soul to you. / I ask you to wear this ring / as a reminder of the vows we have spoken / on this, our wedding day.

❦

3) (Bride/Groom) _____, I give you this ring / as a sign of my commitment and the desire of my heart. / May it always be a reminder / that I have chosen you above all others, / and from this day forward, / we shall be united as husband and wife.

❦

4) (Bride/Groom) _____, as I place this ring on your finger, / may it always remind you of my never-ending love, / and may it always remind me / of the precious treasure I have in you. / Wear this ring with joy, / for your love has made me complete.

❦

5) I give you this ring. / Wear it with love and joy. / As this ring has no end, / neither shall my love for you. / I choose you to be my (wife/husband) / this day and forevermore.

❦

6) This ring I give you / in token of my love and devotion, / and with my heart, / I pledge to you all that I am. / With this ring, I marry you / and join my life to yours.

7) (Bride/Groom) _____, I give you this ring / as a symbol of my love for you. / Just as this band encircles your finger, / may you always feel encircled by my love.

⧢

8) With this ring, I thee wed, / and from this day forward, / I consecrate and commit / my love and my life / to you alone.

⧢

9) You are more precious to me today than yesterday, / and you will be more cherished tomorrow than you are today. / Please wear this ring / as a symbol of my eternal love for you, / a love that transcends all of our yesterdays, / all of our todays, / and all of our tomorrows.

⧢

10) This ring I give in token and pledge / as a sign of my love and devotion. / With this ring, I thee wed.
(Traditional)

⧢

11) (Bride/Groom)_____, I give you my hand as I give you my heart, / unreservedly and unconditionally. / I give you this ring as I give you my love, / exclusively and eternally.

⧢

12) With this ring, I thee wed. / Thou art now my (wife / husband), / my beloved, / my friend. / Whither thou goest, I will go, / and where thou lodgest, I will lodge; / thy people shall be my people, / and thy God, my God. *(Version 1)*

With this ring, I marry you. / You are now my (wife / husband), / my beloved, / my friend. / Where you go, I will go, / and where you live, I will live; / your people will be my people, / and your God, my God. *(Version 2)*

NOTE: Groom's Ring Exchange Vows may be the same as or different from Bride's Ring Exchange Vows.

Prayers and Blessings

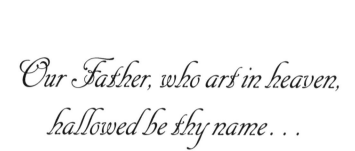

Our Father, who art in heaven,
hallowed be thy name...

PRAYERS AND BLESSINGS

1) Our Father, who art in heaven, hallowed be Thy name. Thy kingdom come, Thy will be done on earth as it is in heaven. Give us this day our daily bread; and forgive us our [debts] trespasses as we forgive [our debtors] those who trespass against us; and lead us not into temptation, but deliver us from evil. For Thine is the kingdom and the power and the glory forever and ever. Amen. *(The Lord's Prayer)*

2) Now you will feel no rain, for each of you will be a shelter for the other. Now you will feel no cold, for each of you will be warmth to the other. Now there will be no loneliness, for each of you will be a companion to the other. Now you are two persons, but there is only one life before you. Go now to your dwelling place to enter the days of your togetherness. May beauty surround you both in the journey ahead and through all the years. May happiness be your companion, and may your days together be good and long upon the earth.

(Apache Blessing)

3) May God bless you [May you be blessed] with Hope enough to keep sunshine in your love, and Fear enough to keep you holding hands in the dark; May God bless you with Unity enough to keep your roots entwined, and Separation enough to keep you reaching for each other; May God bless you with Harmony enough to keep romance in your song, and Discord enough to keep you tuning your love so it becomes sweet music to all who may hear it.

4) Oh Lord, our hearts are filled with joy on this wedding day, as (Groom) _____ and (Bride) _____ come before You pledging their hearts and lives to one another. Grant that they may ever be true and loving, living together in such a way as to never bring shame or heartbreak into their marriage. Temper their hearts with kindness and understanding. Rid them of all pretense and jealousy. Help them to remember to be each other's sweetheart, helpmate, best friend, and guide, so together they may meet the cares and problems of life more bravely. May the home they are creating today truly be a place of love, peace, and harmony, where Your Spirit is always present. Bless this marriage we pray, and walk beside (Groom) _____ and (Bride) _____ throughout their lives together. We ask this in Jesus' name. Amen.

5) God in heaven above, please protect the ones we love. We honour all You created as we [they] pledge our [their] hearts and lives together. We honour mother-earth and ask for our [their] marriage to be abundant and grow stronger through the seasons. We honour fire and ask that our [their] union be warm and glowing with love in our [their] hearts. We honour wind and ask that we [they] sail through life safe and calm as in our [their] Father's arms. We honour water to clean and soothe our [their] relationship that it may never thirst for love. With all the forces of the universe You created, we pray for harmony and true happiness as we [they] forever grow young together. Amen. *(Cherokee Prayer) (May be read by the couple or the Officiant)*

6) May all that you are, always be in love; may all that is love, always be in you. May your love be as beautiful on each day you share as it is on this day of celebration. And may each day you share be as precious to you as the day when you first fell in love. May you always see and encourage the best in each other. May the challenges life brings your way make your marriage even stronger. And may you always be each other's best friend and greatest love.

7) Our Heavenly Father, we ask Your blessing upon these two lives and the home they are establishing today. May the love they have for each other grow deeper and stronger because of their love for You. Lord, You guided them to each other, now guide them in this new journey as husband and wife. As they walk down this path, light their way so they may keep their eyes focused on Your will, their hands holding fast to Your truth, their feet firmly planted in Your Word, and their hearts bound together by Your love. This we pray in Your name. Amen.

8) May these two rings symbolize the spirit of undying love in each of your hearts. Wherever you go, may you always return to one another in your togetherness. May the home you establish be such a place of peace and joy that many will find there a friend. May your love for each other be as a pebble dropped in a pond of water. Like the ripples in the water that cross and recross one another's, may your love touch and retouch all those around you throughout your life together.

9) Dear Lord, we pray that You will bless this man and this woman as they begin their new journey together. In all the experiences of life, may they always stay close to You and to each other as they share the joys and blessings, as well as the trials and heartaches. Help them to honor and keep the promises made here today. Remind them daily of Your great love for them so they, in turn, may reach out in love to others. Give them such love and devotion that each may be to the other a strength in need, a comfort in sorrow, a counselor in difficulty, and a companion in joy. Amen.

10) May your marriage be blessed with faith for the future. May your hearts be filled with the happiness of hope. May your lives be enlightened with an everlasting love. May God grant you a new beginning as He opens the door to life's deepest and richest experiences. May the life you build together be a lasting testimony that a second chance is for those who never give up believing in the power of faith, hope, and love. *(For second marriages)*

11) May God bless your [this] marriage and family as you [they] create a new home together. A family is a circle of strength and love. With every birth and every union, the circle grows. May every joy shared add love to the circle, and may every crisis faced together make the circle even stronger. May your [this] family become like a beautiful rainbow as each color of your [their] lives is carefully blended together with both the showers and the sunshine of God's love. *(For marriages that have children involved in the ceremony)*

12) May the road rise to meet you. May the wind be always at your back. May the sun shine warm upon your face, the rains fall soft upon the fields. May the light of friendship guide your paths together. May the laughter of children grace the halls of your home. May the joy of living for one another trip a smile from your lips, a twinkle from your eye. And when eternity beckons at the end of a life heaped high with love, may the good Lord embrace you with the arms that have nurtured you the whole length of your joy-filled days. May the gracious God hold you both in the palm of His hands. And, today, may the Spirit of Love find a dwelling place in your hearts. Amen. *(Irish Blessing)*

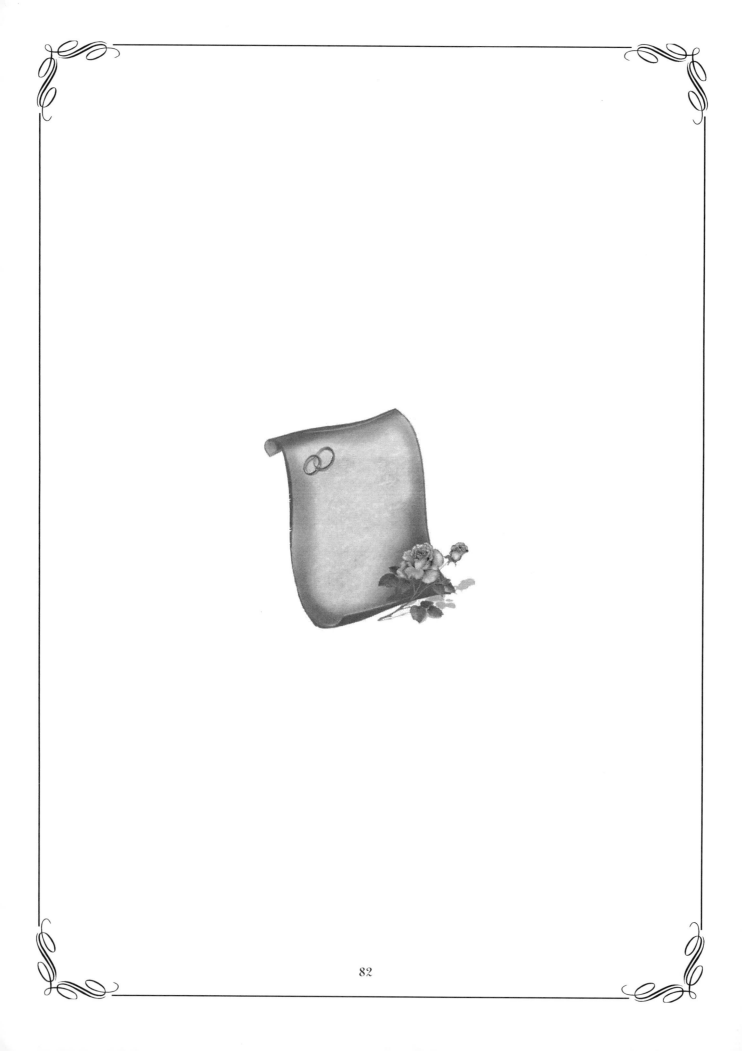

Wedding Traditions
and
Other Special Touches

The Unity Candle is a symbol
of two lives becoming one . . .

Wedding Traditions
and
Other Special Touches

1) Unity Candle

Lighting the Unity Candle symbolizes the joining together or blending of separate lives. It is the coming together of two families and the merging of two individuals into one married couple, a love that burns jointly. The Unity Candle is an arrangement of three candles (the center candle sometimes being larger than the other two). The two side candles are lit either before the wedding ceremony begins or just before the Unity Candle ceremony. These are usually, but not always, lit by the Bride's parents and the Groom's parents on their respective sides of the altar. Lighting the Unity Candle normally takes place after the Bride and Groom exchange vows and rings. The Officiant will share a few thoughts about the unity that exists between a husband and wife when they enter into marriage, after which the couple will take their respective candles and light the center candle. The couple then extinguishes their respective candles by gently blowing out the flame, symbolizing that they are now "one." Sometimes the couple chooses not to blow out their candles to symbolize that, even though they are now one, they continue to retain their individuality. (See words used in Lighting of the Unity Candle in *Traditional, Contemporary, Civil, Short and Sweet, Second Time Around, All in the Family, Interfaith* and *Vow Renewal* ceremonies.)

2) The Marriage Vessel and the Rose®

The Marriage Vessel and the Rose® ceremony may be used as an alternative to the Unity Candle, especially for outdoor weddings. You will need a table for the vessel and the rose. Filling the vessel with water is only necessary if you use the second version. The Officiant begins by explaining the significance of the ceremony.

(The Officiant says):

(Groom) _____ and (Bride) _____ have chosen to share two gifts, The Marriage Vessel and the Rose® , to symbolize their ever-growing lifelong commitment to each other. The spiritual roots of The Marriage Vessel and the Rose® grow out of an understanding of God as the Potter, or Creator of life *(holding up the vessel)*, and God as the Gardener, or Sustainer of life *(holding up the rose)*. The vessel of clay, lovingly shaped by the Potter, is a symbol of love's strength and endurance. Likewise, the rose, born of the tiniest of seeds, symbolizes the beauty and the potential of growing in love throughout life together. The miracle of the vessel is that it not only protects, but is enriched by that which it holds, the rose. Both the vessel and the rose are individually unique, yet when combined, they create an object of even greater beauty.

(Following are two popular versions of The Marriage Vessel and the Rose®.)

The Marriage Vessel and the Rose®

First Version

(The Groom presents the rose to the Bride and says):

(Bride) _____, this rose represents the beauty I see in you. / I thank you for the person you are / and the person I am becoming / because of your love for me.

(The Bride presents the vessel to the Groom and says):

(Groom) _____, this vessel represents the strength I see in you. / I thank you for the love and care you have given me, / and for all we will share together in this life.

(The Bride then places the rose in the vessel; the Bride and Groom hold it together while the Officiant says):

As your gifts bring beauty and purpose to each other, may your lives continue to enrich and strengthen one another.

(The Officiant says):

(Groom) _____ and (Bride) _____, as you share each passing day, and as your days become years, remember this tradition you have created. On each wedding anniversary, place one additional rose in the marriage vessel to symbolize your ever-growing love for one another. May The Marriage Vessel and the Rose® always be a symbol of the beauty and strength you bring to each other's lives.

Second Version

(The Groom hands his Bride a long-stemmed rose and says):

(Bride) _____, take this rose as a symbol of my love. / It began as a tiny bud and blossomed, / just as my love has grown for you.

(The Bride places the rose into a vessel or vase filled with water and says):

(Groom) _____, I take this rose, / a symbol of your love, / and I place it into water, / a symbol of life. / For just as this rose cannot survive without water, / I cannot live without you.

(The Groom responds by saying):

In remembrance of this day, / I will give you a rose each year on our anniversary / as a reaffirmation of my love / and the vows we have spoken here today.

(The Bride responds by saying):

And I will refill this vessel with water each year, / ready to receive your gift / in reaffirmation of the new life you have given me / and the vows we have spoken here today.

(The Bride and Groom join hands around the rose-filled vessel while the Officiant says):

Just as this rose and vessel of water give beauty and life to each other, so may your love blossom and grow throughout your life together.

3) Family Medallion® *(For ceremonies involving children)*

This ceremony, created by Rev. Roger Coleman of Clergy Services, Inc., was designed to significantly include the children of those being married in the wedding celebration. The Family Medallion® provides a symbol for recognizing family relationships by adding a third circle to the two "marriage circles." During this part of the ceremony, the children shall come forward and form a circle with the Bride and Groom who welcome the children into the family and verbally make a commitment to them.

(The Officiant says):

Just as (Groom) _____ and (Bride) _____ gave each other rings as symbols of their love and commitment to one another, they also would like to present [each of] you with a gift as a symbol of their love and commitment to you. The Family Medallion® is made up of three intertwining circles, two of which symbolize the union of this man and woman in marriage. The third circle represents the joining of children to this union, making it complete as we celebrate the new family created here today.

(The Bride and Groom present the children with the Family Medallion®, and give each child a hug and a kiss.)

You may obtain *Family Medallion®* jewelry, at www.lovenotesweddings.com. See the *All in the Family Ceremony* on pages 31-36 for a more expanded presentation of the *Family Medallion®*.

❦

4) Handfasting *(Celtic Tradition)*

The Officiant explains the significance of the handfasting ritual by saying:) Have you ever wondered where the words "tying the knot" come from? The expression "tying the knot" refers to the traditional Celtic marriage ritual of Handfasting. Handfasting is an ancient Celtic word for wedding, and was recognized as a binding contract of marriage between a man and a woman before weddings became a legal function of the government or a papal responsibility of the church. After the wedding vows and ring exchange, the couple's hands were bound together with a cord that was tied in a "love knot," signifying the joining of their lives in a sacred union. Today, handfasting is a symbolic ceremony to honor a couple's desire for commitment to each other, and to acknowledge that their lives and their destinies are now bound together.

(The Officiant holds up the cord and addresses the couple with these words): Please hold each other's hands, palms up *(her hands resting in his)*, so you may see the blessing they are to you. (Groom) _____ and (Bride) _____, this cord is a symbol of the life you have chosen to live together. Up until this moment you have been separate in thought, word, and deed. But as this cord is tied together, so shall your lives become intertwined. With this cord, I bind you to the vows that you have made to one another. With this knot, I tie you heart to heart, together as one.

(The Officiant wraps the cord loosely around the Bride's and Groom's wrists to tie a "love knot" and says): (Groom) _____ and (Bride) _____, the knot of this binding is not bound by the cord, but rather, by your own vows of love. For, as always, you hold in your own hands the making or breaking of this union. May this "love knot" always be a reminder of the binding together of your two hands, two hearts, and two souls into one. And so are you bound, each to the other, for all the days of your lives. *(Cord may then be removed and placed on the altar. Many couples choose to keep the "love knot" as a memento of their new union created that day.)*

NOTE: The Handfasting tradition coordinates well with reading #7, "These Hands" and "Blessing of the Hands."

5) Ceremony of The Rose *(The First Gift)*

First Version

The Ceremony of the Rose symbolizes the merging of the Bride's and Groom's families. When the Bride enters, she has in her possession two roses, usually red. As she approaches the altar, the Bride will stop and offer a rose and a kiss to her mother or significant mother figure. In doing this, she is expressing her gratitude for preparing her for this moment and for receiving the man she is about to marry into her family. When the wedding ceremony has ended and she and the Groom exit, the Bride will stop and offer a rose and a kiss to the Groom's mother or significant mother figure. In doing this, she is expressing her gratitude for preparing her new husband for this moment and for receiving her into the Groom's family. A variation you may consider is to present both roses either upon the entrance or upon the exit.

Second Version

(The Officiant says):

(Groom) _____ and (Bride) _____ have chosen to give each other a rose which is their first gift as husband and wife. *(At this time, the Officiant will give both the Bride and the Groom a rose, and they, in turn, will present their rose to each other.)* This rose was born of the tiniest of seeds and has blossomed into the beautiful flower that it is today. And so it is with your relationship. It began as a small feeling that grew and eventually blossomed into something beautiful. And now you stand before us today to make a commitment to each other as husband and wife. Since you know that love must be shared, it is your desire to share these first gifts with two very special people, two people who helped to prepare you for this moment and molded you into the individuals that you are today. *(The Bride and Groom turn and present their roses to their mothers or significant mother figures and offer a hug or a kiss.)*

Third Version

(The Officiant says):

Today you will receive the most honorable titles that exist between a man and a woman—the titles of husband and wife. You have chosen to give each other a rose as your first gift. In the language of flowers, the rose was considered a symbol of love, and a single rose meant only one thing—"I love you." So it is appropriate that your first gift to each other as husband and wife will be a single rose. Please exchange your gifts. *(The Bride and Groom present each other with a rose.)* (Groom) _____ and (Bride) _____, because you both have given and received this symbol of love, I would encourage you to choose one very special place in your home for roses. Then on each anniversary, you both may take a rose to that special place as a recommitment to your marriage, and express with this symbol that your marriage is a marriage based on love.

In every marriage, there are times when it is difficult to verbalize certain feelings. Sometimes, we hurt those whom we love most, then find it difficult to say, "I am sorry," or "Please forgive me," or "I need you." When you simply cannot find these words, leave a rose at your specially chosen place, and let that rose say what matters most—"I still love you." The other should accept this rose for the words that cannot be found, and remember that the unspoken love is the hope you share and the faith you have in your future together as husband and wife.

6) Unity Cup

First Version

Two separate goblets are filled with wine. Before the couple is pronounced husband and wife, the Officiant pours one-half of the wine from each goblet into a separate cup, the Unity cup, from which each sips.

(The Officiant says): This glass of wine is known as the Unity Cup, or Kiddush Cup, and is symbolic of the Cup of Life. As you share this cup of wine, you share all that the future may bring. The half-filled goblets are a reminder of your individuality; the single cup marks your new life together. As you share the wine from a single cup, so may you, under God's guidance, share contentment, peace, and fulfillment from your own Cup of Life. May you find life's joys heightened, its bitterness sweetened, and each of its moments hallowed by true companionship and love. *(Rabbi's Manual)*

(The Officiant holds up the Unity Cup and may then say this prayer): Blessed are Thou, O Lord our God, Creator of the fruit of the vine. *(The Groom takes a sip of wine first, then offers the cup to the Bride).*

(See the Unity Cup in the *Interfaith Ceremony*).

Second Version

(The Officiant says): As (Groom) _____ and (Bride) _____ share from the Unity Cup, they share in the joy that is created when two people make a lifelong promise to each other. The two small cups represent their two lives. The center cup symbolizes their wish to unite in marriage. *(Family member from each side fills the small cups.)* (Groom) _____ and (Bride) _____, your life has been shaped and filled by your family, so it is a family member who has filled each of your cups. *(Officiant takes an equal portion of wine from each cup and pours it into the Unity Cup and says):* Wine from each cup is added equally to the Unity Cup, symbolizing the equal sacrifice you both happily make to create your marriage.

There are two reasons that not all of the wine in your cups is used. First, this is a reminder that while you are joined together, you continue to be individuals. Your individuality is what first attracted you to each other and what continues to draw you together. So, celebrate your individuality and treasure each other's uniqueness. Second, your family has helped to fill your cup through the years, making you the people you are today, and they will continue to shape your lives. Just as the wine poured by your family remains in your individual cups, so the bond you have with your family will remain as well. In your marriage, as in this wine ceremony, may each of your lives be perfectly combined together *(gesture to Unity Cup)*. And may your individuality remain cherished forever *(gesture to small cups)*. As you share from this Unity Cup, may it be a symbol of your commitment to each other, to your family, and to your marriage. *(The Officiant passes the Unity Cup to the Groom and then to the Bride.)*

7) Breaking of the Glass *(Jewish Tradition)*

The Breaking of the Glass is a Jewish tradition with many meanings. Following are a few of those meanings.

The Breaking of the Glass is:

1) a symbol of the destruction of the Holy Temple in Jerusalem.

2) a reminder of the tragic losses the Jewish people have suffered.

3) a reminder that, even amidst joy, a broken world still needs our attention and people less fortunate still require our care.

4) a reminder not only of sorrow, but also an expression of hope for a future free from all violence and hatred.

5) a representation of the fragility of human relationships.

6) a reminder that marriage changes the lives of individuals forever.

After the couple is pronounced husband and wife, the glass, or light bulb, which usually is wrapped in a cloth and placed in a silk bag, is then laid by the Groom's foot.

(The Officiant says):

We conclude this ceremony with the Breaking of the Glass. In Jewish tradition, the Breaking of the Glass at a wedding is a symbolic prayer and hope that your love for one another will remain until the pieces of the glass come together again, or in other words, that your love will last forever. The fragile nature of the glass also suggests the frailty of human relationships. Even the strongest of relationships is subject to disintegration. The glass then, is broken to "protect" the marriage with this prayer: May your bond of love be as difficult to break as it would be to put the pieces of this glass together again.

The Groom then breaks the glass with his foot and everyone shouts "Mazel Tov!" which means "Good luck and Congratulations!"

Although the glass is shattered, the covering contains the pieces. This represents the difficulties the Bride and Groom may face together, but which will remain contained by the unity they have created this day.

This tradition usually takes place sometime after the pronouncement, either right before or right after the kiss. (See the Breaking of the Glass in the *Interfaith Ceremony*.)

8) **Bible, Coins, and Lasso** *(la Biblia, las Arras, y el Lazo—Hispanic Tradition)*

The Bible, Coins, and Lasso (la Biblia, las Arras, y el Lazo) are Hispanic traditions most often associated with the Catholic Church and Mexican weddings, although Spain and other Latin-American countries use variations of these, as well. They are symbolic of the spiritual, physical, and emotional elements in a marriage. The Bible symbolizes the religious guidance and wise counsel for life's decisions—spiritual element. The thirteen coins, like a dowry, represent the financial support and blessings for their home—physical element. The lasso signifies the union of their hearts, souls, and lives into one common destiny—emotional element.

Bible (la Biblia)—Spiritual

After the Bride and Groom exchange their vows and rings, Sponsors, or Padrinos, bring forth a white Bible and a Rosary and place it in the hands of the Bride and Groom. *(While they are holding it, the Officiant will bless the Bible with these words):* Lord, bless this Bible and the lives of those who read it. We know that the Holy Bible is the Word of God. We pray that it will be the spiritual guide that will light your pathway and will guide you in all your decisions, so that your will and God's will are one and the same. Amen. *(The Sponsors then take the Bible and Rosary and sit down.)*

Coins (las Arras)—Physical

The Coin Sponsors bring forth the box of coins and empty it into the Groom's hands. *(The Officiant, explaining their significance, says):* These thirteen coins are a symbol of the care that the Bride and Groom will give in order for their home to have everything it needs. These coins also are a sign of the blessings of God and all the good things they will share together. *(The Officiant then blesses the coins with these words):* Lord, may these coins be a symbol of mutual help throughout their lives. Provide them with all they need for their home. We give You thanks for all the good things they are going to share because of Your many blessings. Amen.

The Groom drops the coins into the Bride's hands and says the following vows: (Bride) _____, receive these thirteen coins as a symbol of my dedication in caring for our home and providing for our family's necessities.

The Bride responds by saying: (Groom) _____, I accept your gift of dedication, and I promise on my part that everything provided will be used with care for the benefit of our home and family. *(The Sponsors then take the coins and sit down.)*

Lasso (el Lazo)—Emotional

Lastly, the Lasso Sponsors bring forth the lasso and place it around the shoulders of the kneeling Bride and Groom in a figure eight, which symbolizes eternity. *(The Officiant then blesses their union with these words):* (Groom) _____ and (Bride) _____, this lasso symbolizes the union of two hearts into one heart, two souls into one soul, and two lives into one life. O Lord, bless this couple as they journey through life together . . . hand in hand, heart to heart, flesh to flesh, and soul to soul. Amen. *(The Sponsors then remove the lasso and sit down.)*

(See la Biblia, las Arras, y el Lazo in the *Bilingual Traditional Ceremony*.)

9) **Jumping the Broom** *(African-American Tradition)*

The tradition of "Jumping the Broom" symbolizes sweeping away the old and welcoming the new—a symbol of a new beginning.

The ceremony begins (oftentimes to the sound of the beating of traditional African drums) with the guests forming a circle around the Bride and Groom as they stand in front of the broom on the floor. The couple picks up the broom and begins to sweep around in a circle while the Officiant explains the symbolism.

(The Officiant says): "Jumping the broom" may have its roots in an African tribal marriage ritual where sticks were placed on the ground, representing the couple's new home. However, it became popular among African-American slaves who could not legally marry, so they created their own rituals to honor their unions. The broom was chosen because it has been the household symbol of "home" throughout history. It also has been said that the spray of the broom symbolizes the scattering of the African race, and the handle represents the Almighty, who holds them all together.

(The Officiant then says): The Bride and Groom are sweeping together in a circle to signify the "sweeping away" of their former single lives, their past problems and their previous cares. The broom represents a threshold between past and present, and "jumping the broom" symbolizes the crossing of this threshold into a new relationship as husband and wife. Starting a new life with another person does require a "leap of faith," and by taking this leap, the couple shows their dedication to work together through all of life's circumstances.

The Bride and Groom then place the broom on the floor and join hands as the drums beat louder and faster. Everyone counts, "One, two, three . . . jump!" After they jump, the Officiant may conclude the ceremony with this version of a traditional slave poem:

> Dark and stormy may come the weather,
> This man and woman are joined together.
> Let none but Him that makes the thunder,
> Put this man and woman asunder.
> I therefore announce you both the same,
> Be good, go long, and keep up your name.
> The broomstick's jumped, the world's not wide,
> She's now your own, go kiss your bride!

This custom may take place during the ceremony after the couple is pronounced "husband and wife," or at the reception just after the bridal party enters the reception area.

Many couples choose to decorate their broom with ribbons, flowers, shells, feathers, beads or other mementos to make it unique as a special keepsake for their home.

Sometimes a "double broom" is used during the ceremony, symbolizing the joining of two households into one. *(The Officiant would then say):* This double broom represents the two homes from which the Bride and Groom came, now joined together into one, symbolizing the new home that is created here this day.

10) **Blessing Stones** *(Wishing Stones)*

The ritual of the Blessing Stones, or Wishing Stones, as they sometimes are called, is a wonderful way to include everyone in the wedding by way of offering blessings and good wishes to the newlyweds. It also is a good way to ensure that everyone will make contact with the Bride and Groom at some point during the day. This ritual may be performed at the actual ceremony itself (before the blessing), or at the conclusion of the service (in a receiving line manner), or later at the reception.

When the guests arrive at the ceremony, they are given a Blessing Stone along with a note card with words printed on it such as: "My wish for you is . . ." or "May you be blessed with . . ." or "May God bless you with . . ."

During the ceremony, the Officiant explains the significance of the Blessing Stones. *(The Officiant says):* Today is a very blessed occasion in the lives of (Groom) _____ and (Bride) _____ . You have been invited here today because of your special relationship with them. When you arrived, you received a stone along with a notecard. These are called "Blessing Stones." Since we all desire nothing but the best that life has to offer this couple, I ask each of you to complete the sentence on the card and sign your name, so your best wishes and your blessings for (Groom) _____ and (Bride) _____ may always be a reminder of your love for them on this day of celebration.

At some point (either during or after the service), the guests will share their blessing or wish with the newlyweds and toss the Blessing Stone into a Blessing Bowl, a Wishing Well, a Fountain, or whatever is chosen to hold the water. They then may place their "love note" into a basket or box for the couple to reflect on at a later time. Many couples keep their Blessing Stones in a special place in their home (a vase of flowers, around a candle, in an aquarium, etc.) to remind them of all the love, good wishes, and blessings they share because of their family and friends.

A variation of this ritual would be at an outdoor wedding near a body of water (lake, pond, ocean, etc.). Stones either are gathered at the site or provided for the guests. After the ceremony, everyone follows the Bride and Groom's recessional to the water, makes a wish or blessing for them and casts their stone into the water.

(The Officiant says:) The ripples that are made in the water represent the love and good wishes not only for this couple, but for all the world. For as our ripples cross and recross one another's, so our love and good wishes touch and retouch all those around us and all those with whom we come into contact throughout our lives. (This also may be said at the indoor ceremony.)

You can be as creative as you want with this ritual. Here are some ideas:

♥ Stones—you may use decorative stones, rose quartz stones, which symbolize love, or other pebbles from a special place.

♥ Container for water—you will need a Blessing Bowl (any decorative basin, bowl, or bucket will work), or a table top fountain, or a Wishing Well (as large and elaborate or as small and simple as you wish).

♥ Love Notes—buy decorative, ready-made note cards from a stationery or craft store and print your opening blessing phrase on them, or, for an even more personal touch, design and print your own note cards at home on your computer. Remember to begin your blessing phrase with: "My wish for you is . . ." or "May you be blessed with . . ." or "May God bless you with . . ."

11) Blending of the Sands *(Hawaiian Tradition)*

The Blending of the Sands is a beautiful and meaningful unifying ceremony from Hawaii that symbolizes the joining together of the Bride and Groom or the blending together of their families. There are two versions offered—one for the couple and one for the family.

Glass containers are needed for the Bride, Groom, and each child represented (when children are included). Each container is filled with a different colored sand, representing each individual's uniqueness. *(Optional: the Officiant also may hold a vase filled with sand. He may begin the sand ceremony by pouring a layer of neutral colored sand into the Unity Sand Vase, which symbolizes the foundation of the marriage.)* After the Officiant reads the sand ceremony text, the Bride and Groom (and each child) pour their individual containers of sand into the Unity Sand Vase. They may wish to leave a small amount of sand in each container to symbolize that, although they now are joined as one, they still retain their own individuality.

Version 1—The Couple
(The Officiant says): (Groom) _____ and (Bride) _____, today you are making a commitment to share the rest of your lives with each other. Your relationship is symbolized through the pouring together of these two individual containers of sand. (Groom) _____, through the sands of time you have grown into the person you are today. This container of sand represents all that you were, all that you are, and all that you will ever be. (Bride) _____, through the sands of time you have grown into the person you are today. This container of sand represents all that you were, all that you are, and all that you will ever be. As you each hold your separate container of sand, it symbolizes your lives prior to this moment; individual and unique. Now as you blend the sands together, it symbolizes the blending together of your two hands, two hearts, and two lives into one. *(The Bride and Groom combine their sands into the Unity Sand Vase.)* Just as these grains of sand can never be separated again, so may your lives be blended together for all eternity.

Version 2—The Family
(The Officiant says): (Groom) _____, (Bride) _____, and (Children) _____ _____, today you are making a commitment to share the rest of your lives with each other. Your new family relationship is symbolized through the pouring together of these individual containers of sand. One represents you, (Groom) _____, and all that you are as husband and father. One represents you, (Bride) _____, and all that you are as wife and mother. The other container(s) represent(s) (Children) _____ who make(s) this family complete. As you each hold your separate container of sand, it symbolizes your lives before today. Now as you blend the sands together, it symbolizes the blending together of your hands, your hearts, and your lives into one family. *(The Groom, Bride, and Children combine their sands into the Unity Sand Vase.)* Just as these grains of sand can never be separated again, so may your lives be blended together for all eternity.

Creative ideas:
- ♥ The Unity Sand container, as well as the individual containers, may be a vase, vial, bottle, jar, heart-shaped, or any other shape glass container.
- ♥ Choose a color of sand that reflects your unique personality.
- ♥ Melt some wax to seal the Unity Sand Vase, which also will hold the sand in place, and then seal it with a cork or a lid.
- ♥ Have your names, initials or wedding date etched into the glass of the Unity Sand Vase for a special wedding keepsake and a reminder of your union.

12) **The Attendant Pendant**® *(For special recognition of the Bridal Party)*

(*The Officiant says*): Oftentimes at a wedding celebration, the bridesmaids and groomsmen are overlooked because the focus is mainly on the Bride and Groom. However, (Groom) _____ and (Bride) _____ want everyone here to know how much you mean to them. You have been asked to stand up with them as their attendants to witness the most important event of their lives (Groom's) _____ friends who stand with him today have always been there for him, just as (Bride's) _____ friends have always been there for her. That is what friends do. Friends are always there for you through the good times and the bad. Friends are always there to listen to you. They do not judge, they do not condemn, they do not criticize. Instead, they support, they encourage, they challenge. The Bible says, "A friend loves at all times." It also has been said that "a true friend is one who walks in when the rest of the world walks out."

Outside of the marriage and family relationship, there is no greater bond that exists than that of the bond of friendship. And so, (Groom) _____ and (Bride) _____ would like to present each of you with a friendship gift. (*At this point, the Bride and Groom may present each attendant with their friendship gift.*) This gift is a specially designed keepsake called the Attendant Pendant®. The Attendant Pendant® design is created in the shape of a circle, which signifies the "circle of love" that exists between friends. Within this larger circle are two smaller circles, each holding a heart. The two hearts represent the Bride and Groom. The two circles that encompass the hearts represent the Bride's and Groom's individual circle of friends. You can see that the two hearts are intertwined, signifying the joining of two best friends, the Bride and Groom, in the bonds of marriage. But notice that their individual circles are linked together, as well, symbolizing that the bonds of friendship also are being woven together in such a way that his friends and her friends now have become their friends. Let me share a poem about friendship that expresses the feelings the Bride and Groom have for each one of you.

Circle of Friends
Love is a circle, no beginning and no end. It keeps us together like our Circle of Friends.
But the gift of love I want you to see is the treasure of friendship you have given to me.
Our bonds are strong and cannot be broken. Because of our friendship, this oath must
be spoken:
    When you are sad, I will dry your tears. When you are scared, I will comfort your fears.
    When you are worried, I will give you hope. When you are confused, I will help you cope.
    When you are lost and can't see the light, I shall be your beacon, shining ever so bright.
This is my oath, I pledge till the end. "Why?" you may ask.
    Because you are my Friend.

Whenever you look at your Attendant Pendant®, may it always remind you of this day of celebration and the special bonds of love that forever tie you to this circle of friends.

(To order the Attendant Pendant®, go to www.lovenotesweddings.com.)

(The Groom/Bride says): All of you have come here today because you are very special to (Bride/Groom) _____ and me. Our wedding would not be complete without you here, and we have asked you to stand up with us because you are our closest friends. Sometimes the bridesmaids and groomsmen get lost in the wedding celebration because the focus is on the Bride and Groom. But we want you to know that it is an honor for us to have you here to share in our special day. We have been through a lot together. My friends have always been there for me, just as I know (Bride's/Groom's) _____ friends have always been there for her/him. (Optional: The Bible says that "A friend loves at all times," and you certainly have demonstrated that in our lives.)

We want everyone to know just how much you mean to us. So, (Bride/Groom) _____ and I have something we would like to give you. We want this to be not only a reminder of our wedding, but also a reminder of how special your friendship is to us. *(At this point, the Bride and Groom present each attendant with their friendship gift.)* *(The Groom/Bride then says)*: This is our friendship gift to you. It is a specially designed keepsake called the Attendant Pendant®. The Attendant Pendant® design is created in the shape of a circle, which signifies the "circle of love" that exists between friends. Within this larger circle are two smaller circles, each holding a heart. The two hearts represent two best friends, (Bride/Groom) _____ and me. Each heart is encompassed by its own circle, which represents (Bride's/Groom's) _____ individual circle of friends and my individual circle of friends. You can see that the two hearts are intertwined, signifying the joining of our hearts in the bonds of marriage. But notice that the individual circles are linked together, as well, symbolizing that the bonds of friendship also are being woven together. (Bride's/Groom's) _____ friends and my friends now have become our friends. Let me share a poem about friendship that expresses the feelings (Bride/Groom) _____ and I have for each one of you.

Circle of Friends
Love is a circle, no beginning and no end. It keeps us together like our Circle of Friends.
But the gift of love I want you to see is the treasure of friendship you have given to me.
Our bonds are strong and cannot be broken. Because of our friendship, this oath must
be spoken:
    When you are sad, I will dry your tears. When you are scared, I will comfort your fears.
    When you are worried, I will give you hope. When you are confused, I will help you cope.
    When you are lost and can't see the light, I shall be your beacon, shining ever so bright.
This is my oath, I pledge till the end. "Why?" you may ask.
    Because you are my Friend.

Whenever you look at your Attendant Pendant®, may it always remind you of this day of celebration and the special bonds of love that forever tie you to this circle of friends.

(To order the Attendant Pendant®, go to www.lovenotesweddings.com.)

Wedding Ceremony Formations

Groom, Best Man, and Groomsmen enter
Bridesmaids and Maid of Honor enter
Ring Bearer and Flower Girl enter
Bride enters

Processional Formation #1

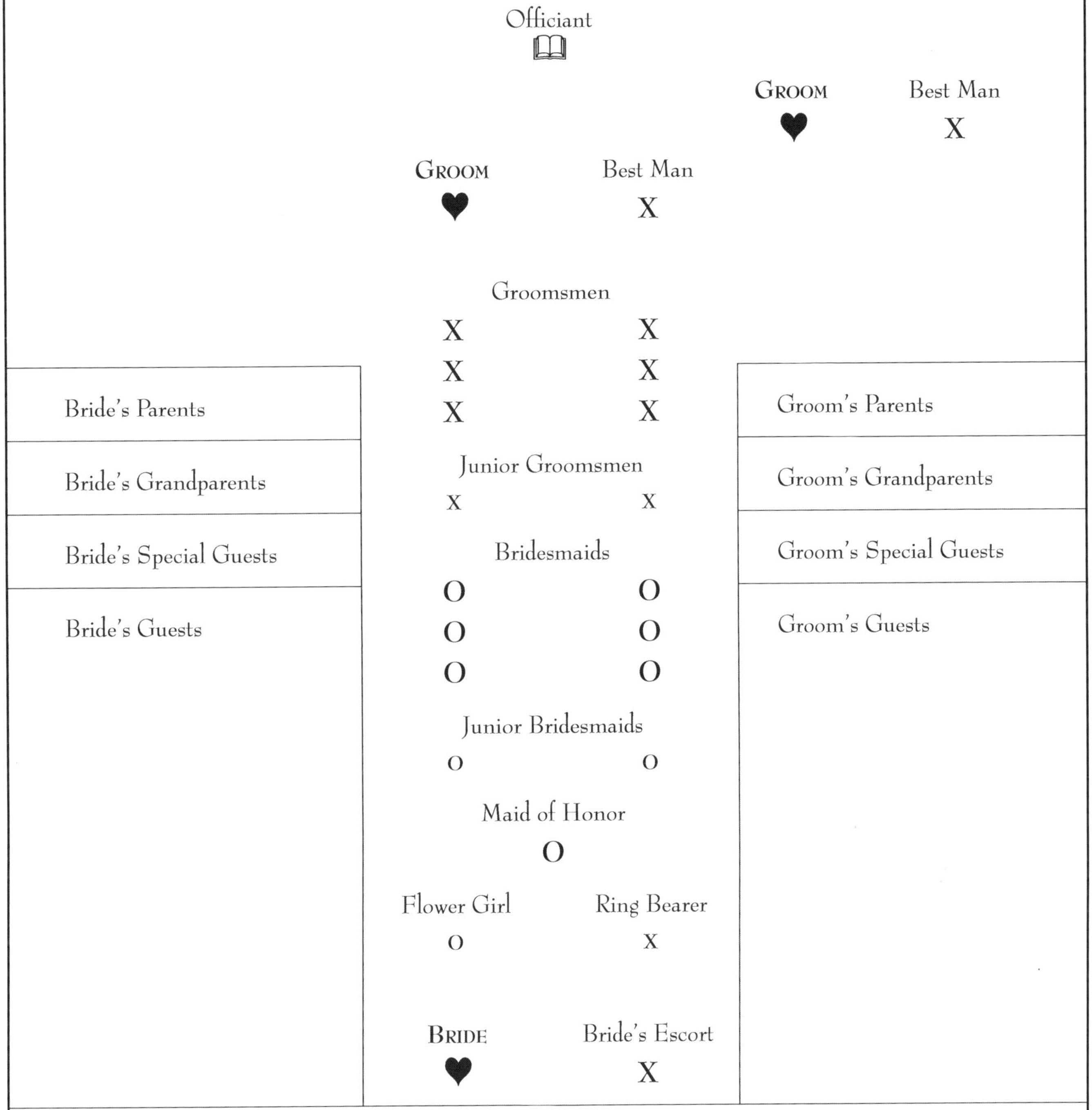

Officiant

Bride's Parents | Groomsmen | Groom's Parents

GROOM ♥   Best Man X

GROOM ♥   Best Man X

Groomsmen

X   X

X   X

X   X

Bride's Parents   Groom's Parents

Junior Groomsmen

X   X

Bride's Grandparents   Groom's Grandparents

Bridesmaids

O   O

O   O

O   O

Bride's Special Guests   Groom's Special Guests

Bride's Guests   Groom's Guests

Junior Bridesmaids

O   O

Maid of Honor

O

Flower Girl   Ring Bearer

O   X

BRIDE ♥   Bride's Escort X

Processional Formation #1

Groom and Best Man enter together from back or front.
Groomsmen and Junior Groomsmen enter in pairs.
Bridesmaids and Junior Bridesmaids enter in pairs.
Maid of Honor enters alone.
Flower Girl and Ring Bearer enter together or single file.
Bride enters with Escort.

Processional Formation #2

Officiant
📖

Groom
♥

Best Man
X

Groom
♥

Best Man
X

Groomsmen
X
X
X

Bride's Parents	Groomsmen	Groom's Parents
Bride's Grandparents		Groom's Grandparents
Bride's Special Guests		Groom's Special Guests
Bride's Guests		Groom's Guests

Bridesmaids
O
O
O

Maid of Honor
O

Ring Bearer
X

Flower Girl
O

BRIDE   Bride's Escort
♥   X

Processional Formation #2

Groom and Best Man enter together from back or front.
Groomsmen enter single file.
Bridesmaids enter single file.
Maid of Honor enters alone.
Flower Girl and Ring Bearer enter together or single file.
Bride enters with Escort.

Processional Formation #3

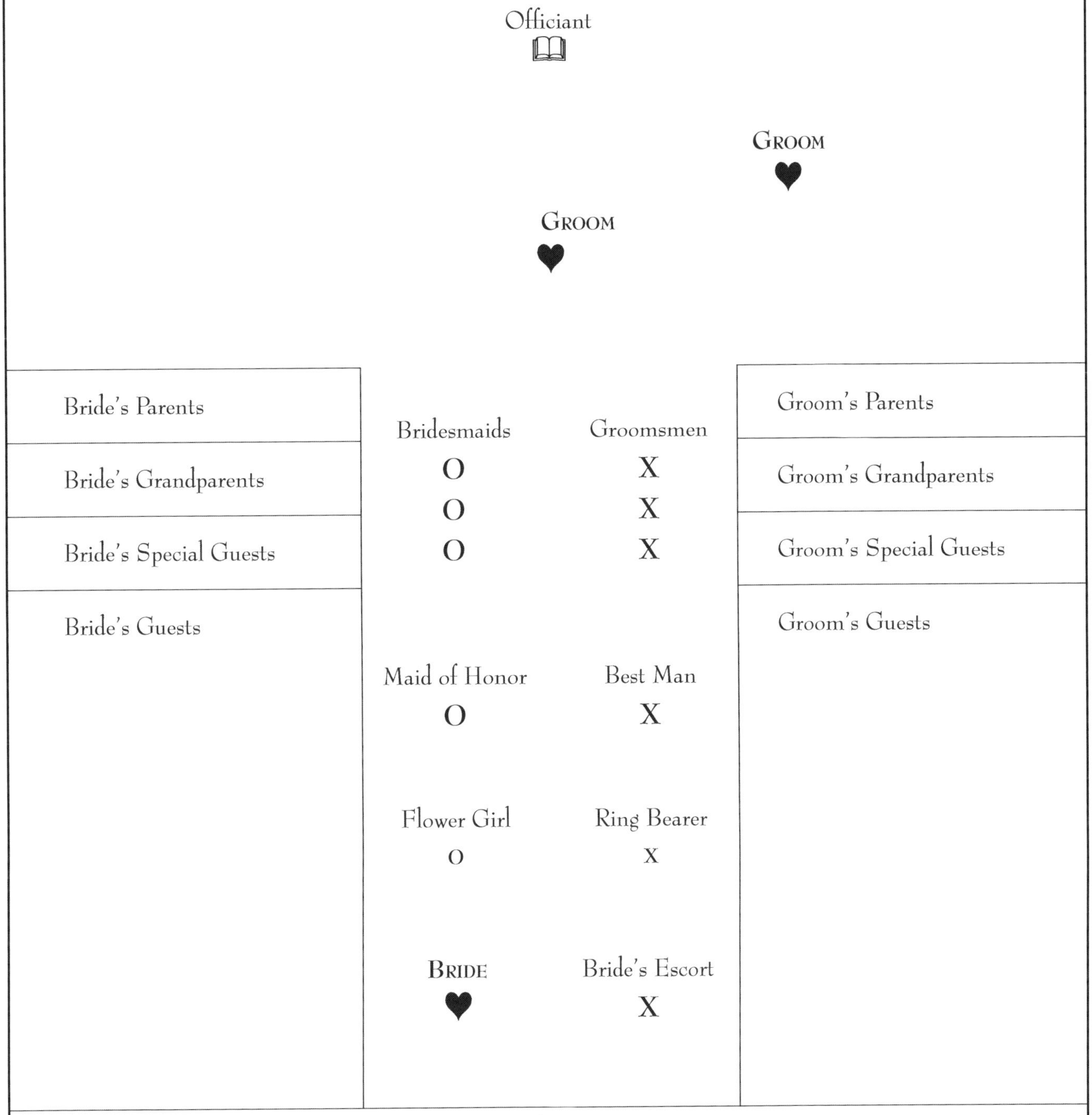

Officiant
📖

GROOM
♥

GROOM
♥

Bride's Parents	Bridesmaids	Groomsmen	Groom's Parents
Bride's Grandparents	O	X	Groom's Grandparents
	O	X	
	O	X	
Bride's Special Guests			Groom's Special Guests
Bride's Guests			Groom's Guests
	Maid of Honor	Best Man	
	O	X	
	Flower Girl	Ring Bearer	
	o	X	
	BRIDE	Bride's Escort	
	♥	X	

Processional Formation #3

Groom enters alone from back or front.
Bridesmaids and Groomsmen enter as couples.
Maid of Honor and Best Man enter as a couple.
Flower Girl and Ring Bearer enter together.
Bride enters with Escort.

Processional Formation #4

Officiant
📖

GROOM   Best Man
♥   X

Bride's Parents	GROOM ♥	Best Man X	Groom's Parents
Bride's Grandparents			Groom's Grandparents
	Bridesmaids	Groomsmen	
Bride's Special Guests	O	X	Groom's Special Guests
	O	X	
Bride's Guests	O	X	Groom's Guests

Maid of Honor
O

Flower Girl   Ring Bearer
O   X

BRIDE   Bride's Escort
♥   X

Processional Formation #4

Groom and Best Man enter together from back or front.
Bridesmaids and Groomsmen enter as couples.
Maid of Honor enters alone.
Flower Girl and Ring Bearer enter together.
Bride enters with Escort.

Processional Formation #5

Officiant

GROOM   Best Man   Groomsmen

♥   X   X   X   X

Bride's Parents	Bridesmaids	Groom's Parents
	O	
Bride's Grandparents	O	Groom's Grandparents
	O	
Bride's Special Guests		Groom's Special Guests
	Maid of Honor	
Bride's Guests	O	Groom's Guests

Ring Bearer

X

Flower Girl

O

BRIDE   Bride's Escort

♥   X

Processional #5

Groom, Best Man, and Groomsmen enter from front.
Bridesmaids enter single file.
Maid of Honor enters alone.
Flower Girl and Ring Bearer enter together or single file.
Bride enters with Escort.

Processional Formation #6
(Jewish)

Rabbi   Cantor

✡   ♪

Groomsmen

X

X

X

Best Man

X

Groom's Parents	Groom's Father **GROOM** Groom's Mother X ♥ O	Bride's Parents
Groom's Grandparents	Bridesmaids O O O	Bride's Grandparents
Groom's Special Guests	Maid of Honor O	Bride's Special Guests
Groom's Guests	Ring Bearer Flower Girl X O Bride's Father **BRIDE** Bride's Mother X ♥ O	Bride's Guests

Processional Formation #6

Groomsmen and Best Man enter single file from back.
Groom enters with Parents.
Bridesmaids and Maid of Honor enter single file.
Flower Girl and Ring Bearer enter together or single file.
Bride enters with Parents.

Altar Formation #7

Officiant

BRIDE   GROOM
♥   ♥

Maid of Honor   Best Man
O

O

Bridesmaids   O   O   x   X   X   Groomsmen

O   Flower Girl   Ring Bearer   X

O   X

O   X

Bride's Parents	Groom's Parents
Bride's Grandparents	Groom's Grandparents
Bride's Special Guests	Groom's Special Guests
Bride's Guests	Groom's Guests

Altar Formation #7

Bride and Groom stand in center.
Maid of Honor and Best Man stand beside and slightly behind Bride and Groom.
Bridesmaids and Groomsmen fan out and down diagonally from Maid of Honor and Best Man.
Flower Girl stands between Bride and Maid of Honor.
Ring Bearer stands between Groom and Best Man.

Altar Formation #8

Officiant

Maid of Honor   Best Man

O   X

BRIDE   GROOM

♥   ♥

Groomsmen and Bridesmaids   Bridesmaids and Groomsmen

X   O   O   x   O   X

Flower Girl   Ring Bearer

X   O   O   X

Bride's Parents		Groom's Parents
Bride's Grandparents		Groom's Grandparents
Bride's Special Guests		Groom's Special Guests
Bride's Guests		Groom's Guests

Altar Formation #8

Bride and Groom stand in center.
Maid of Honor and Best Man stand beside and slightly in front of Bride and Groom.
Bridesmaids and Groomsmen stand as couples and fan out and down diagonally.
Flower Girl and Ring Bearer stand beside and slightly behind Bride and Groom.

Altar Formation #9

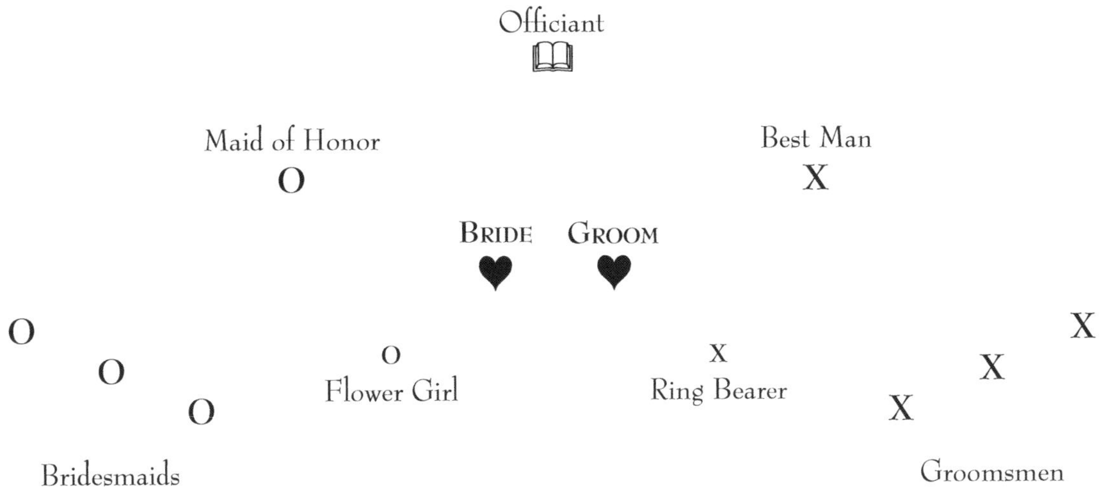

Officiant

📖

Maid of Honor

O

Best Man

X

BRIDE **GROOM**

♥ ♥

O

O

O

O
Flower Girl

X
Ring Bearer

X

X

X

X

Bridesmaids

Groomsmen

Bride's Parents		Groom's Parents
Bride's Grandparents		Groom's Grandparents
Bride's Special Guests		Groom's Special Guests
Bride's Guests		Groom's Guests

Altar Formation #9

Bride and Groom stand in center.
Maid of Honor and Best Man stand beside and slightly in front of Bride and Groom.
Bridesmaids and Groomsmen stand diagonally inward.
Flower Girl and Ring Bearer stand beside and slightly behind Bride and Groom.

Altar Formation #10
(Jewish)

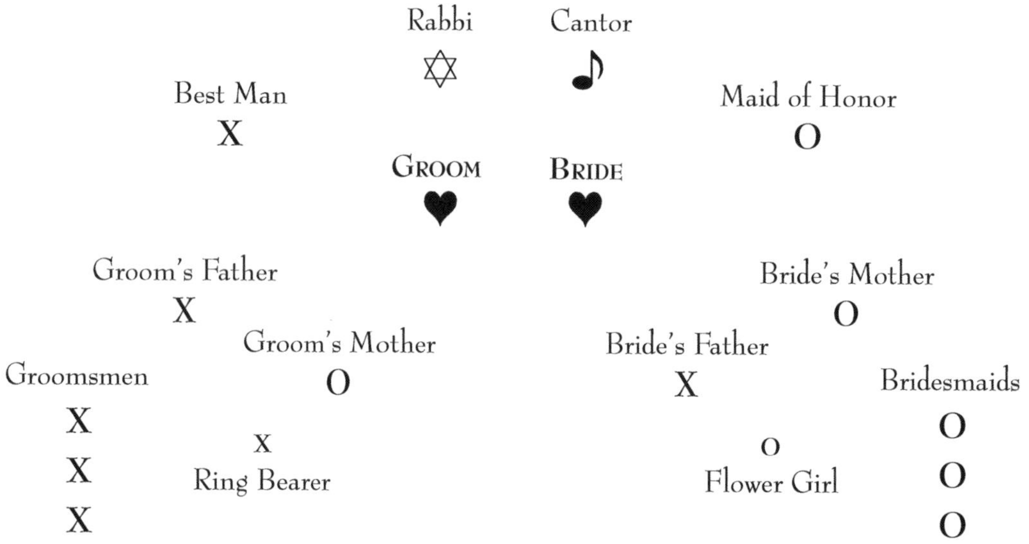

Rabbi   Cantor

✡   ♪

Best Man   Maid of Honor

X   O

GROOM **BRIDE**

♥   ♥

Groom's Father   Bride's Mother

X   O

Groom's Mother   Bride's Father

O   X

Groomsmen   Bridesmaids

X   O

X   x   o   O

X Ring Bearer   Flower Girl O

Groom's Parents		Bride's Parents
Groom's Grandparents		Bride's Grandparents
Groom's Special Guests		Bride's Special Guests
Groom's Guests		Bride's Guests

Altar Formation #10

Bride and Groom stand in center.

Maid of Honor and Best Man stand beside and slightly in front of Bride and Groom.

Bridesmaids and Groomsmen stand in a vertical straight line.

Flower Girl and Ring Bearer stand next to Bridesmaids and Groomsmen.

Parents of Bride and Groom stand between couple and attendants or may be seated.

Recessional Formation #11

Officiant

Bride's Parents	Groom's Mother O	Groom's Father X	Groom's Parents
Bride's Grandparents	Bride's Mother O	Bride's Father X	Groom's Grandparents
Bride's Special Guests	Bridesmaids O O O	Groomsmen X X X	Groom's Special Guests
Bride's Guests	Junior Bridesmaid O	Junior Groomsman X	Groom's Guests
	Maid of Honor O	Best Man X	
	Flower Girl O	Ring Bearer X	
	Bride ♥	Groom ♥	

Recessional Formation #11

Bride and Groom exit first.
Flower Girl and Ring Bearer exit second.
Maid of Honor and Best Man exit third.
Junior Bridesmaid and Junior Groomsman exit fourth.
Bridesmaids and Groomsmen exit fifth.
Bride's Parents exit sixth and Groom's Parents exit last.

Recessional Formation #12
(Jewish)

Rabbi   Cantor

Groom's Parents	Groomsmen	Bridesmaids	Bride's Parents
	X	O	
Groom's Grandparents	X	O	Bride's Grandparents
	X	O	
Groom's Special Guests	Best Man	Maid of Honor	Bride's Special Guests
	X	O	
Groom's Guests	Ring Bearer	Flower Girl	Bride's Guests
	X	o	
	Groom's Father	Groom's Mother	
	X	O	
	Bride's Father	Bride's Mother	
	X	O	
	GROOM	BRIDE	
	♥	♥	

Processional Formation #12

Bride and Groom exit first.
Bride's Parents exit second.
Groom's Parents exit third.
Flower Girl and Ring Bearer exit fourth.
Maid of Honor and Best Man exit fifth.
Bridesmaids and Groomsmen exit last.

Wedding Ceremony
Order of Service

Processional
Exchange of Vows and Rings
Wedding Blessing
Pronouncement
Recessional

Wedding Ceremony Order of Service

Prelude Music *(20-30 minutes before ceremony begins)*
Lighting of Candles
Seating of Groom's Grandparents
Seating of Bride's Grandparents
Seating of Groom's Parents
Seating of Bride's Mother / Parents
Musical Selection *(optional)*
Processional begins
Officiant, Groom and Groomsmen enter
   (Officiant and Groom only, if Groomsmen enter with Bridesmaids)
Bridesmaids enter
Maid/Matron of Honor enters
Ring Bearer and Flower Girl enter
Bride enters on Escort's left arm
Welcome/Invocation
Consent of the Bride and Groom
Presentation of the Bride *(Escort takes his seat)*
Address and Readings by the Officiant *(Others may participate in readings)*
Musical Selection *(optional)*
Wedding Vows
Explanation of the Rings
Ring Exchange Vows
Lighting of the Unity Candle *(or other Wedding Tradition)*
Musical Selection *(optional)*
Wedding Prayer/Blessing
Musical Selection *(optional)*
Pronouncement of Marriage
Kiss
Presentation of the Couple—(Mr. and Mrs.) _____
Recessional begins
Groom and Bride exit
Ring Bearer and Flower Girl exit
Groomsmen and Bridesmaids exit together
Bride's Parents are escorted out
Groom's Parents are escorted out
Bride's Grandparents are escorted out
Groom's Grandparents are escorted out
Officiant makes announcements, dismisses the guests, then exits

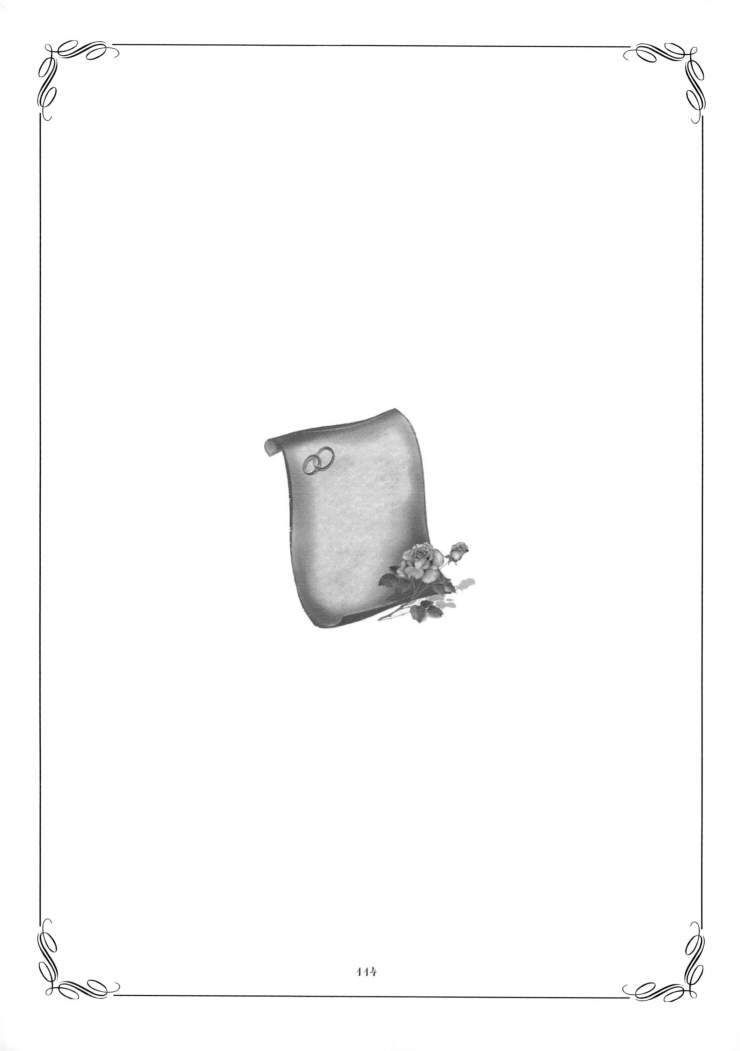

Wedding Program Samples

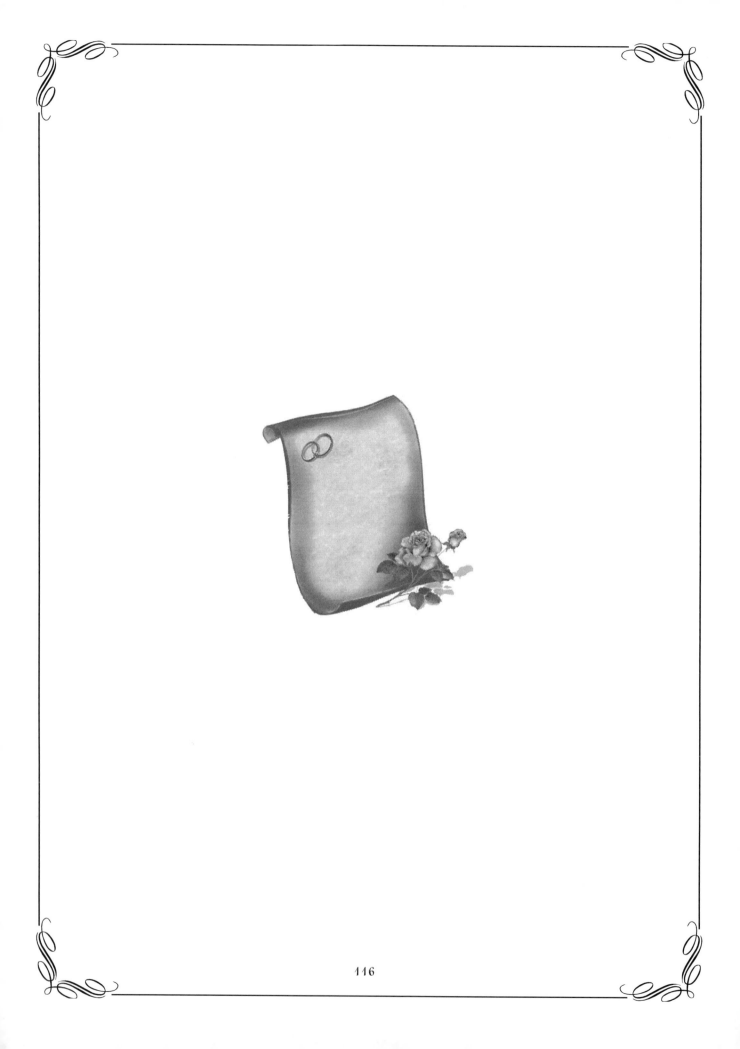

WEDDING PROGRAM
SAMPLE I

Musical Prelude

Lighting of the Candles

Seating of the Parents

Solo—*Sunrise, Sunset*   Bock

Processional

    Canon in D   Pachelbel

    Bridal Chorus   Wagner

Welcome/Invocation

Consent of the Bride and Groom

Giving Away of the Bride

Address

Reading—The Love Chapter, I Corinthians 13

Wedding Vows

Explanation of the Rings

Exchange of the Rings

Reading—These Hands

Lighting of the Unity Candle

Duet—*God, a Woman and a Man*   Green

Wedding Prayer

Pronouncement of Marriage

Kiss

Presentation of the Couple

Recessional

    The Wedding March   Mendelssohn

WEDDING PARTY
SAMPLE I

Minister
Rev. Marty Younkin

| **Parents of the Bride** | **Parents of the Groom** |
| Mr. & Mrs. Robert Armstrong | Mr. & Mrs. Dale Workman |

Parents of the Bride
Mr. & Mrs. Robert Armstrong

Parents of the Groom
Mr. & Mrs. Dale Workman

Grandparents of the Bride
Mrs. Gloria Baker

Grandparents of the Groom
Mr. & Mrs. Anton Dideriksen

Maid of Honor
Jeane Armstrong

Best Man
Robert Harms

Bridesmaids
Linda Armstrong
Beth Schmidt

Groomsmen
Craig Johnson
Jerry Workman

Junior Bridesmaid
Jaime Lin Moser

Junior Groomsman
Dan Tipton

Flower Girl
Ashlyn Moser

Ring Bearer
Zachary Moser

Readers
Jim Workman
Gail Workman

Ushers
Jeff Workman
John Workman

Organist
Arline Moser

Violinist
Bud Moser

Vocalists
Tina Moser
Sarah Moser

WEDDING PROGRAM
SAMPLE II

Prelude   Carol Sage, Pianist

Seating of the Family

    The Wedding Song (Stookey)   Dave Shaw, Soloist

Processional

    Jesu, Joy of Man's Desiring (Bach)   Attendants' Procession

    Trumpet Voluntary in D (Clarke)   Bride's Procession

Welcome

Consent

Presentation of the Bride

Address and Readings   The Honorable Brian Nichols

Exchange of the Vows and Rings

Family Medallion® Ceremony

Reading

    The Happy Home Recipe   Alan and Donna Ackles, Readers

Family Unity Candle

    Love Will Be Our Home (Chapman)   Marlene Bickel and Marilyn Giese, Duet

Marriage Blessing

Pronouncement

Presentation of the Couple and New Family

Recessional

    Joyful, Joyful, We Adore Thee (Beethoven)

Wedding Party
Sample II

Parents
Bud and Arline Moser .... Parents of the Bride
Delano and Mildred Younkin .... Parents of the Groom

Matron of Honor
Cheryl DiMarzio .... Friend of the Couple

Best Man
Don Younkin .... Brother of the Groom

Bridesmaids
Carissa Younkin .... Daughter of the Groom
Judy Moser .... Sister-in-law of the Bride

Groomsmen
Charlton Younkin .... Son of the Groom
Clayton Younkin .... Son of the Groom

Flower Girl
Elizabeth Moser .... Cousin of the Bride

Ring Bearer
Brandon Moser .... Cousin of the Bride

Ushers
David Moser .... Brother of the Bride
Scott Moser .... Nephew of the Bride
Brian Moser .... Nephew of the Bride

Readers
Alan and Donna Ackles .... Friends of the Couple

Musicians
Carol Sage, Pianist .... Friend of the Couple
Dave Shaw, Vocalist .... Friend of the Couple
Marlene Bickel, Vocalist .... Sister of the Groom
Marilyn Giese, Vocalist .... Sister of the Groom
Ted Giese, Trumpeter .... Brother-in-law of the Groom

Officiant
The Honorable Brian Nichols .... Friend of the Couple

WEDDING PROGRAM
SAMPLE III

Prelude Music

Seating of the Parents/Grandparents   *Wind Beneath My Wings*

Attendants' Processional   *Unchained Melody*

Bride's Processional   *Portrait of My Love*

Invocation

Declaration of Intent

Minister's Address to the Couple

Pledging of Wedding Vows

Giving of Rings

Marriage Vessel and Rose® Ceremony   *The Rose*

Wedding Blessing

Pronouncement of Marriage

Presentation of the Couple

Recessional   *We've Only Just Begun*

WEDDING PARTY
SAMPLE III

Parents of the Bride
Ms. Dixie Shaffer   Mr. & Mrs. Carroll Shaffer

Parents of the Groom
Mr. & Mrs. Bob Boatright   Mr. Alan Ackles

Grandparents of the Bride
Mrs. Betty Shaffer

Grandparents of the Groom
Mr. & Mrs. Gene Ackles

Maid of Honor
Brenda Lewis

Best Man
Tony DiMarzio

Bridesmaids
Dana Boatright   Darla Shaffer

Groomsmen
Wendell Eads   Bobby Hibbitts

Flower Girl
Donna Burley

Ring Bearer
Preston Burley

Ushers
Charlton Younkin   Clayton Younkin

Minister
Rev. Char Schultz

Musicians
Janice Gibson, Soloist   Kathy Hart, Harpist

Wedding Rehearsal Worksheets

Practice Makes Perfect!

Wedding Rehearsal Information Worksheet

Date of Rehearsal _____ Time of Rehearsal _____

Location of Rehearsal _____

Phone No.(_____) _____ Number of Wedding Guests _____

Wedding Party

Bride _____ Groom _____

Maid of Honor _____ Best Man _____

Bridesmaids _____ Groomsmen _____

_____ _____

_____ _____

_____ _____

_____ _____

Jr. Bridesmaid _____ Jr. Groomsman _____

Flower Girl(s) _____ Ring Bearer(s) _____

_____ _____

Ushers *(light candles / seat family members)*

_____ _____

Family Members

Bride's Parents _____ Groom's Parents _____

_____ _____

Grandparents _____ Grandparents _____

_____ _____

Bride's Children _____ Groom's Children _____

_____ _____

Wedding Personnel

Officiant _____ Sound Technician _____

Coordinator _____ Photographer _____

Musicians _____ Videographer _____

DJ / Band _____ Florist _____

Order of Ceremony Worksheet

Pre-Wedding Pictures taken at _____ a.m./p.m.

Pre-Wedding Music begins at _____ a.m./p.m. by _____

Candles lit by _____

Musical Selection for seating of Parents/Grandparents _____

Groom's Grandparents seated on right by _____

Bride's Grandparents seated on left by _____

Groom's Parents seated on right by _____

Bride's Mother seated on left by _____

Aisle cloth positioned by ushers _____ and _____

Wedding Processional begins

Musical Selection for Bridal Party Entrance _____

Musical Selection for Bride's Entrance _____

Wedding Processional Formation (circle one)   #1   #2   #3   #4   #5   #6   other (diagram)

Altar Formation (circle one)   #7   #8   #9   #10   other (diagram)

Wedding Ceremony begins

    Welcome/Invocation

    Consent of the Bride and Groom

    Presentation of the Bride

    Address and Readings by the Officiant

    Musical Selection (optional) _____

    Wedding Vows

    Explanation of the Rings

    Ring Exchange Vows

    Lighting of the Unity Candle (or other Wedding Tradition)

    Musical Selection (optional) _____

    Wedding Prayer/Blessing

    Musical Selection (optional) _____

    Pronouncement of Marriage

    Kiss

    Presentation of the Couple

Wedding Recessional begins

Musical Selection for Exit _____

Wedding Recessional Formation (circle one)   #11   #12   other (diagram)

Bride's Parents ushered out by _____

Groom's Parents ushered out by _____

Bride's Grandparents ushered out by _____

Groom's Grandparents ushered out by _____

Officiant makes appropriate announcements and dismisses guests

NOTE: When applicable, Stepparents will be seated according to the Bride's and Groom's wishes.

REHEARSAL QUESTIONS WORKSHEET

Complete all diagrams. *(See Processional, Recessional, and Altar Formation Worksheets-pages 129-131)*

1. Formal Names *(used at beginning of ceremony)*
   Bride _____   Groom _____

   Familiar Names *(used during remainder of ceremony, if different from above)*

   Bride _____   Groom _____

   Bride's Children _____   Groom's Children _____

   _____   _____

2. Maid/Matron of Honor   Best Man

   _____   _____

   Bridesmaids *(in order)*   Groomsmen *(in order)*

   _____   _____
   _____   _____
   _____   _____
   _____   _____
   _____   _____

   Enter ❑ as couples? ❑ single file? In what order? *(See Processional Formation Diagram-page 129)*
   Where do they stand? *(See Altar Formation Diagram-page 131)*
   How do the men stand? ❑ Tin soldier? ❑ Parade rest? ❑ Fig leaf? *(left hand over right)* ❑ Other?

3. Ring Bearer(s)

   _____   _____

   Flower Girl(s)

   _____   _____
   _____   _____

   Enter ❑ together? ❑ single file? *(See Processional Formation Diagram-page 129)*
   Where do they stand? *(See Altar Formation Diagram-page 131)* or ❑ Seated with Adult?

4. Parents   Escort
   (B) _____   _____

   (G) _____   _____

   Grandparents   Escort
   (B) _____   _____

   (G) _____   _____

5. Where are Parents, Grandparents and special guests seated? *(See Processional Formation Diagram-page 129)*

6. Candelabras? ❏ Yes ❏ No
   Who lights candles? _____ When? _____

7. Aisle cloth? ❏ Yes ❏ No
   Who will roll it out? _____ When? _____

8. Who is Bride's Escort? _____
   Escort's response for presentation of the Bride? _____

9. Does veil cover face? ❏ Yes ❏ No
   Who lifts the veil? _____ When? _____

10. Vows will be ❏ read by Bride and Groom? ❏ repeated after Officiant?

11. Who has wedding rings?
    ❏ Ring Bearer? ❏ Best Man? ❏ Maid of Honor? ❏ Officiant? ❏ Other?

12. Unity Candle? ❏ Yes ❏ No
    Who lights two side candles? _____ When? _____
    Side candles will ❏ remain lit through ceremony? ❏ be extinguished once center candle is lit?
    Musical selection for Unity Candle _____

13. Other musical selections during ceremony? ❏ Yes ❏ No
    Selection _____ Seating of Parents/Grandparents
    Selection _____ Bridal Party Entrance
    Selection _____ Bride's Entrance
    Selection _____ Bridal Party Exit
    Selection _____ Other _____

14. Other wedding traditions or special touches? ❏ Yes ❏ No
    Selection _____ When? _____
    Selection _____ When? _____
    Selection _____ When? _____

15. Family/Friends participate in readings? ❏ Yes ❏ No
    Selection _____ By whom? _____
    Selection _____ By whom? _____

16. How shall Officiant introduce you during presentation at end of ceremony?
    _____

17. In what order does Bridal Party exit? *(See Recessional Formation Diagram-page 130)*

18. Parents and Grandparents ❏ escorted out? ❏ dismissed by row? ❏ remain seated for pictures?
    Guests dismissed ❏ row by row? ❏ all at one time? ❏ remain seated?

19. Return for photographs? Bridal Party? ❏ Yes ❏ No Family Members? ❏ Yes ❏ No

20. Announcements: _____
    _____

Processional Formation Worksheet

Processional Formation Worksheet

Use this rehearsal worksheet diagram for placement of guests, family members, and Bridal Party for the Processional Formation. Insert names if desired.
(See Processional Formations #1-6 on pages 97-102 for reference.)

Key: ♥ - Bride and Groom   X - Men
       📖 - Officiant   O - Women

Recessional Formation Worksheet

Recessional Formation Worksheet

Use this rehearsal worksheet diagram for placement of guests, family members, and Bridal Party for the Recessional Formation. Insert names if desired.
(See Recessional Formations #11-12 on pages 107-108 for reference.)

Key: ♥ - Bride and Groom   X - Men
       📖 - Officiant   O - Women

Altar Formation Worksheet

Altar Formation Worksheet

Use this rehearsal worksheet diagram for placement of guests, family members, and Bridal Party for the Altar Formation. Insert names if desired.
(See Altar Formations #7-10 on pages 103-106 for reference.)

Key: ♥ - Bride and Groom   X - Men
      📖 - Officiant   O - Women

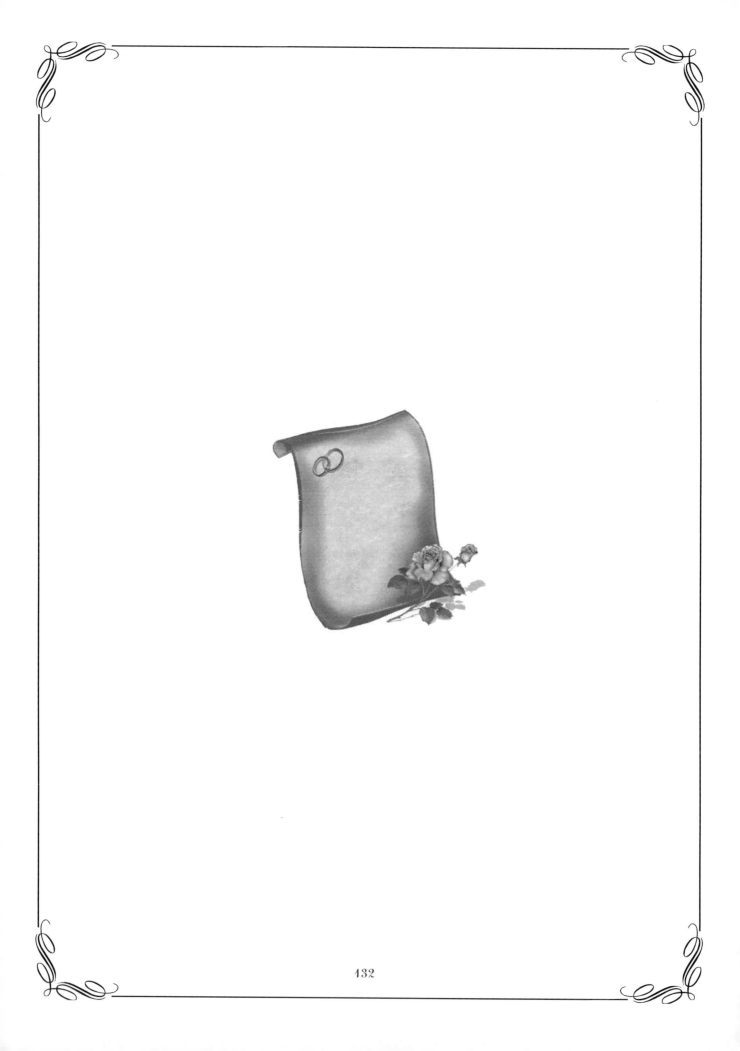

Personalized Wedding Ceremony Worksheets

Choose the perfect words
for the perfect wedding!

Personalized Wedding Ceremony Worksheet

Option One: Select a complete ceremony <u>exactly</u> as written:

COMPLETE CEREMONY *(Select ceremony exactly as written)*

_____ Traditional   _____ Short and Sweet   _____ Interfaith
_____ Contemporary   _____ Second Time Around   _____ Bilingual
_____ Civil   _____ All in the Family   _____ Vow Renewal

———— OR ————

Option Two: Personalize your Wedding Ceremony by choosing the following:
All ceremonies are represented throughout the options as shown.

WELCOME *(Choose one)*

_____ Traditional   _____ Short and Sweet   _____ Interfaith
_____ Contemporary   _____ Second Time Around   _____ Bilingual
_____ Civil   _____ All in the Family   _____ Vow Renewal

CONSENT *(Choose one)*

_____ Traditional   _____ Short and Sweet   _____ Interfaith
_____ Contemporary   _____ Second Time Around   _____ Bilingual
_____ Civil   _____ All in the Family   _____ Vow Renewal

ADDRESS *(Choose one)*

_____ Traditional   _____ Short and Sweet   _____ Interfaith
_____ Contemporary   _____ Second Time Around   _____ Bilingual
_____ Civil   _____ All in the Family   _____ Vow Renewal

READINGS *(Choose as many as desired)*

_____ #1 *(Second Time Around)*   _____ #5   _____ #9
_____ #2 *(Civil)*   _____ #6 *(Interfaith)*   _____ #10 *(All in the Family)*
_____ #3 *(Traditional)*   _____ #7   _____ #11 *(Traditional, Bilingual)*
_____ #4 *(Short and Sweet)*   _____ #8 *(Vow Renewal)*   _____ #12 *(Traditional, Bilingual, Contemporary, Second Time Around)*
    (version 1 or 2)

WEDDING VOWS *(Choose one for Bride (B); one for Groom (G)—may be the same or different)*

_____ #1 *(Contemporary)*	_____ #5	_____ #9 *(All in the Family)*
_____ #2 *(Civil)*	_____ #6 *(Short and Sweet)*	_____ #10
_____ #3 *(Interfaith)*	_____ #7	_____ #11
_____ #4 *(Vow Renewal)*	_____ #8 *(Second Time Around)*	_____ #12 *(Traditional, Bilingual)*

EXPLANATION OF THE RINGS *(Choose one)*

_____ Traditional	_____ Short and Sweet	_____ Interfaith
_____ Contemporary	_____ Second Time Around	_____ Bilingual
_____ Civil	_____ All in the Family	_____ Vow Renewal

RING EXCHANGE VOWS *(Choose one for Bride (B); one for Groom (G)—may be the same or different)*

_____ #1 *(Short and Sweet)*	_____ #5 *(Civil)*	_____ #9 *(Vow Renewal)*
_____ #2 *(Contemporary)*	_____ #6 *(Civil)*	_____ #10 *(Traditional)*
_____ #3 *(Contemporary)*	_____ #7 *(Second Time Around)*	_____ #11
_____ #4 *(All in the Family)*	_____ #8 *(Bilingual)*	_____ #12 *(Interfaith)*
		(version 1 or 2)

LIGHTING OF THE UNITY CANDLE *(Choose one)*

_____ Traditional	_____ Short and Sweet	_____ Interfaith
_____ Contemporary	_____ Second Time Around	_____ Bilingual
_____ Civil	_____ All in the Family	_____ Vow Renewal
	(option A or B or C)	

PRAYERS AND BLESSINGS *(Choose one)*

_____ #1	_____ #5	_____ #9 *(Contemporary)*
_____ #2 *(Civil)*	_____ #6 *(Vow Renewal)*	_____ #10 *(Second Time Around)*
_____ #3 *(Short and Sweet)*	_____ #7 *(Traditional, Bilingual)*	_____ #11 *(All in the Family)*
_____ #4	_____ #8	_____ #12 *(Interfaith)*

PRONOUNCEMENT *(Choose one)*

_____ Traditional	_____ Short and Sweet	_____ Interfaith
_____ Contemporary	_____ Second Time Around	_____ Bilingual
_____ Civil	_____ All in the Family	_____ Vow Renewal

WEDDING TRADITIONS AND OTHER SPECIAL TOUCHES *(Choose as many as desired)*

_____ #1 Unity Candle

_____ #2 The Marriage Vessel and the Rose®
      (version 1 or 2)

_____ #3 Family Medallion®

_____ #4 Handfasting *(Celtic)*

_____ #5 Ceremony of the Rose *(The First Gift)*
      (version 1 or 2 or 3)

_____ #6 Unity Cup
      (version 1 or 2)

_____ #7 Breaking of the Glass *(Jewish)*

_____ #8 Bible, Coins, & Lasso *(Hispanic)*
      (la Biblia, las Arras, y el Lazo)

_____ #9 Jumping the Broom *(African-American)*

_____ #10 Blessing Stones *(Wishing Stones)*

_____ #11 Blending of the Sands *(Hawaiian)*
      (version 1 or 2)

_____ #12 Attendant Pendant®
      (Ceremony or Rehearsal Dinner version)

WEDDING CEREMONY FORMATIONS *(Choose one from each category)*

Processional		Altar		Recessional	
_____ #1	_____ #4	_____ #7	_____ #9	_____ #11	
_____ #2	_____ #5	_____ #8	_____ #10	_____ #12	
_____ #3	_____ #6				
_____ other		_____ other		_____ other	

SPECIAL INSTRUCTIONS *(See "Special Ceremony Instructions" page 138)*

❑ Yes   ❑ No

PERSONAL TOUCH *(Optional—See "A Personal Touch" page 139 if you want this included in your ceremony)*

❑ Yes   ❑ No

SPECIAL CEREMONY INSTRUCTIONS

Include any special instructions for the Officiant, i.e., notes on special wording, participation of family or friends in ceremony, names of Bride's and Groom's children involved in the Celebration of the New Family ceremony, seating arrangements, placement of musical selections, secrets from or surprises for Bride, Groom, or family members, etc.

A Personal Touch

If you would like the Officiant to include in your wedding ceremony anything "personal" about your relationship, please respond to any of the following questions/statements you consider appropriate. Remember: Answer these only if you wish this to be included in your ceremony.

1) Briefly describe how you met. _____
   _____
   _____
   _____
   _____
   _____

2) What attracted you to each other? _____
   _____
   _____
   _____
   _____
   _____

3) Describe your proposal. _____
   _____
   _____
   _____
   _____

4) Is there anything humorous or interesting that has happened in your relationship that you would like the Officiant to share during the ceremony?
   _____
   _____
   _____
   _____
   _____

NOTES

Use this page for notes or questions you may have, or be creative and write your own vows.

ACKNOWLEDGMENTS

To Carol Moser Sage-Younkin, my partner and best friend:

Thank you so much for being my sounding board in pursuing this project. It was your love, moral support, and encouragement that made this endeavor possible. Your editorial skills, undaunted efforts, and endless dedication made this book a reality. Thank you for believing in me. I love you.

To Craig Bunch:

Thank you for helping me get started on this project. You were always there when I needed you, and I am grateful to you for helping me become somewhat computer literate.

To Beth Schmidt of B&Jdesign:

Is there anything you can't do? You perfected this book from cover to cover. We thank God for your abilities as a graphic designer, but we especially are thankful for the friendship we developed during this project. We will be eternally indebted to you—literally!

To Milli Brown and staff at Brown Books:

Thank you for your encouragement, flexibility, and expertise in bringing this project to completion—finally!

We also would like to acknowledge the following individuals for the use of their writings:

Claire Cloninger	Stephen T. Fader	Wilferd A. Peterson
Roger Coleman*	Matthew Henry	Kenneth W. Phifer
Dorothy R. Colgan	Edmund O'Neill	Carol Sage
Roy Croft	Anne Peterson***	Diane Warner**

*The Marriage Vessel and the Rose® ceremony (first version) reprinted with permission from Roger Coleman, Clergy Services, Inc., 706 West 42nd St., Kansas City, MO 64111

**A Rose Ceremony (second version) reprinted, with permission of the publisher, from The Complete Book of Wedding Vows: Hundreds of Ways to Say I Do, ©1996 by Diane Warner. Published by Career Press, Franklin Lakes, NJ. All rights reserved.

***I'd Marry You Again reprinted with permission from Anne Peterson, author, speaker and poet. For more information about Anne Peterson's ministry, go to www.annepeterson.com.

To order the Family Medallion®, go to www.lovenotesweddings.com.

To order the Attendant Pendant®, go to www.lovenotesweddings.com.

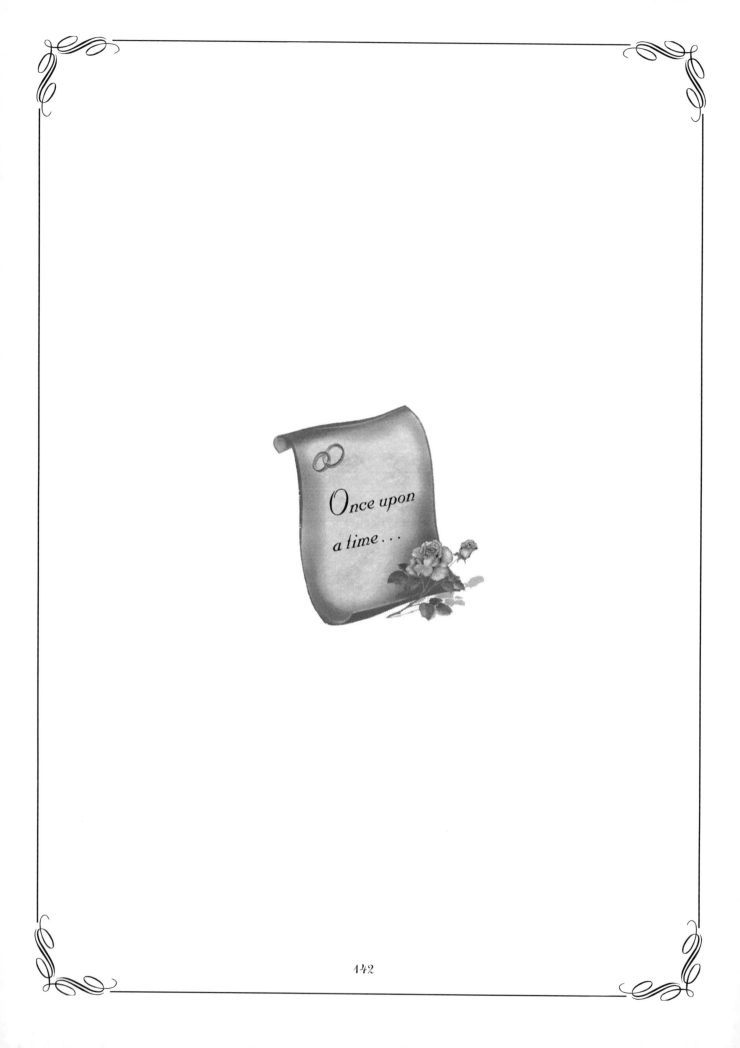

Once upon
a time . . .

ABOUT THE AUTHOR

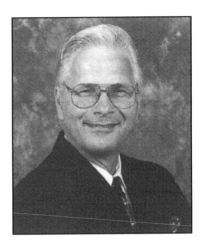

Rev. Marty Younkin

Rev. Marty Younkin, affectionately known as "Minister Marty, the Marryin' Man," has tied the knot for thousands of couples for more than 30 years. He has a Masters of Divinity degree from Dallas Theological Seminary and was a Singles Pastor for many years until he worked himself out of a job by marrying off the singles and turning them into couples.

Rev. Younkin is the Founder and Executive Director of Love Notes-Dallas/Ft. Worth Clergy Services in Dallas, TX. Love Notes is a highly respected organization of non-denominational ministers and officiants who provide ministerial services for weddings, vow renewals, memorial services, baptisms, child dedications, etc. Love Notes fills the need for people who do not have a connection with a place of worship or who do not personally know a minister, priest, rabbi or judge who can perform these services for their special event.

Marty Younkin is married to his bride and best friend, Carol Sage Younkin, with whom he collaborated in writing this book. They have three children and live in the Dallas metroplex.

His advice for a successful marriage?

To keep your marriage brimming
In the loving cup
Whenever you're wrong—admit it.
Whenever you're right—shut up!

...*And they lived happily ever after!*

ORDER FORM

To order additional copies of *A Wedding Ceremony to Remember*, complete the information below:

Ship to: *(please print)*

Name: _____

Address: _____

City, State, Zip: _____

Day Phone: (_____) _____

_____ copies of *A Wedding Ceremony to Remember* at $19.95 each $ _____

Texas Residents must include sales tax $ _____

Postage and handling at $5.00 per book $ _____

Total amount enclosed $ _____

*Make checks payable to **Love Notes** and send to:*

Love Notes
P.O. Box 852071
Richardson, TX 75085-2071

www.lovenotesweddings.com

ORDER FORM

To order additional copies of *A Wedding Ceremony to Remember*, complete the information below:

Ship to: *(please print)*

Name: _____

Address: _____

City, State, Zip: _____

Day Phone: (_____) _____

_____ copies of *A Wedding Ceremony to Remember* at $19.95 each $ _____

Texas Residents must include sales tax $ _____

Postage and handling at $5.00 per book $ _____

Total amount enclosed $ _____

*Make checks payable to **Love Notes** and send to:*

Love Notes
P.O. Box 852071
Richardson, TX 75085-2071

www.lovenotesweddings.com

Made in the USA
San Bernardino, CA
30 January 2017